GUIDE TO

ADOLESCENT ENRICHMENT

A COMPLETE
TEEN ISSUES / SELF-ESTEEM PROGRAM

Used as a Companion Tool to

WHY CAN'T ANYONE HEAR ME?

by Monte Elchoness, Ph.D.

MONROE PRESS
Sepulveda, California

Library of Congress Cataloging in Publication Data

Elchoness, Monte
      Why can't anyone hear me?
      Bibliography: p.
      Includes index.
      1. Adolescence.   2. Adolescent psychology.
      3. Parent and Child.   I. Title
HQ796.E523   1986   305.2'35   86-737
ISBN 0-936781-01-7 (pbk.)
ISBN 0-936781-02-5 (Guide to Adolescent Enrichment)

Printed in the United States of America

I proudly dedicate this book with love to my three-month-old grandson Daniel Charles Bardwil, a future teen-ager who already reflects a keen awareness and astute interest in life and the world in which he lives. The pleasure Daniel provides serves as a reminder that we are all born to give and receive love.

FOREWORD and ACKNOWLEDGMENTS

Self-esteem plays a major role in the direction young people take in their lives. Improving how they feel about themselves involves much more than working on a singular issue. There is a need, in my opinion, for teen programs that can encourage preteens and teens to explore the many issues they now are exposed to, or will soon be facing.

This *Guide to Adolescent Enrichment*, along with its text *Why Can't Anyone Hear Me?* provide a complete curriculum for implementing a Teen Issues/Self-Esteem Program in your school, church or adolescent counseling group. By offering guidance at this time in young people's lives, they will be better prepared to face their future in a more positive way. Through this non-threatening learning process with their peers, these young people first learn to express how they feel about and relate to the characters and events of *Why Can't Anyone Hear Me?* Then they learn to think about and express their feelings concerning the many issues that affect their lives. This is an action-oriented program that asks young people to think, feel, write about, and share feelings, but it also guides them to take action to improve their lives. The results produced by this program, through the young people's efforts, could well bring about an improvement in how they see and value themselves.

My special thanks to Gail Quinn and Chris Humphrey for their able and willing assistance. In creating this *Guide* I feel fortunate in having received their valuable input. As dedicated teachers, they, like myself, realize the importance of reaching young people early and providing them with the skills they require for facing life in a positive way.

I would also like to express my deep appreciation to Norma Caylin, a loving friend, and to Dorothy Towvim, senior editor at Monroe Press. With their able guidance and editorial assistance, this project became manageable and enjoyable as well.

The cover illustration for this *Guide* was prepared by Helena Bowerman.

CONTENTS

PREFACE

This *Guide* was written for educators and counselors like yourself who have devoted their professional careers to helping young people during their critical periods of growth. A number of you, in addition to providing me with positive feedback on *Why Can't Anyone Hear Me?*, have requested an instructional guide to facilitate using this book's materials in a structured setting. Wanting to be responsive to these requests and my own desire to reach and help a greater number of our youth, has motivated me to set aside my other tasks to provide this *Guide to Adolescent Enrichment*.

The development of this *Guide* has evolved into a comprehensive Teen Issues/Self-Esteem Program, which goes far beyond the scope originally conceived. In its broader focus, this *Guide* covers the many aspects of a young person's life and addresses all of these topics in depth.

Helping young people, although difficult at times, is extremely important to us all. The guidance they receive is not only beneficial to them and their future but to the future of our society as well.

INTRODUCTION

Includes Use of the Guide

For adults, communicating with teens is often a frustrating task. As might be expected, young people claim it's not easy for them either. They complain that adults don't understand them. Unfortunately, there may be some truth in what they say. The physical and emotional changes that take place in the adolescent during this period of growth are often trying on everyone, including the young person.

The purpose of the *Guide to Adolescent Enrichment*, in conjunction with *Why Can't Anyone Hear Me?*, is to provide you with the structure and tools for developing a complete Teen Issues/Self-Esteem Program. As teachers and counselors you will help these teens and preteens become more hopeful about their future, feel better about themselves, learn to improve their communication skills, and better understand the changes within themselves. Through group involvement, these young people explore and gain an understanding of the positive options available to them and how to implement these options.

As difficult as it might be to get teens to open up with anyone other than their peers, it is essential to their well-being that this learning start. As a therapist, I realize how guarded many people are and how fearful it is for them to talk about their feelings. We all feel better after sharing some of the so-called "stuff" we carry around inside of us. Young people are no different than adults; if they are in a trusting environment that is nonjudgmental, the sharing becomes easier for them.

Why Can't Anyone Hear Me? was written to hold young people's interest while providing them with information and guidance. Through the characters and events in its story, they are able to relate to what takes place, and in a non-threatening way they learn to improve their communication skills and relationships with adults. One of the major goals of *Why Can't Anyone Hear Me?*, which becomes more easily implemented through this *Guide*, is helping young people view themselves and their lives in a more hopeful and positive way.

Teens often grow tired of hearing adults lecture them. They quickly learn how to do selective listening. This *Guide* has been prepared with that in mind. Utilizing the many experiences from *Why Can't Anyone Hear Me?*, this *Guide* offers group and individual experiences young people can enjoy while at the same time helping them become more in touch with themselves and others. These exercises, while designed to encourage sharing, should not be used to force interaction.

As a rule, personal experiences are best shared in a safe environment where a trusting bond or connection with others exists. An important goal of this *Guide* and your program is to create such an environment. As a word of caution, it must be remembered that because every young person is unique, they each carry their own history of experiences which affects them differently. These differences must be respected in regard to an individual's ability to join into the sharing exercises. We all grow at our own pace; therefore, personal growth must not be forced upon another, especially in a group setting.

In creating a safe environment, I refer to the need for considering the comfort zone of the individual. People feel comfortable when they are able to relate to or have something in common with someone else. That is the basis for the strength teens feel in their peer group connection. Conversely, when teens lack that feeling of connection with adults, they also feel they have nothing at all in common with them. Their comfort zone, which fosters open communication, is then affected.

One method for bridging that gap between security and communications for teens and adults is through the paradigm of storytelling and metaphors. Utilizing the characters in *Why Can't Anyone Hear Me?* and their situations provides the common base or link for making relating easier. As the scary feelings teens often experience when talking about themselves are reduced, they may actually find that sharing becomes enjoyable. Through this approach, learning becomes an integral part of the relating and sharing process.

My hope is that in working with *Why Can't Anyone Hear Me?* and the *Guide to Adolescent Enrichment*, you find this process will help young people to discover more positive paths for themselves through the adventures of their adolescence and beyond.

USE OF THE GUIDE

The format for this *Guide* is both consistent and easy to apply. Each chapter in the *Guide* refers to the events and characters in the corresponding chapter of *Why Can't Anyone Hear Me?* (the text) and uses the same chapter titles. Every chapter in the *Guide* includes:

> Contents page showing exercise topics
>
> Summary of the text chapter
>
> Significant points
>
> Exercise objective for each significant point
>
> Leader's notes for each exercise
>
> Exercises, located at the end of each chapter (also in *Student Workbook*)

Each text chapter from *Why Can't Anyone Hear Me?* should be assigned for home reading prior to being discussed in class.

INFORMATION ON THE EXERCISES

The exercises are varied, including multiple choice, true or false, brainstorming, consensus, journal writing, sentence completion, matching and answering questions. Exercises are worked independently, in small groups, and within the whole group. They are all, with the exception of the personal journal writing, shared through discussion by the whole group at the conclusion of the exercise. For the journal exercises, anyone desiring to share any part of this activity can do so, but it is not to be required of them. The exercises serve as the catalyst for the most significant part of the group activity, interaction through discussion and sharing. Through this interaction the cohesiveness of the group develops, the individuals gain a freedom of expression, and there is movement toward self-awareness and growth.

STUDENT/PARTICIPANT WORKBOOK

Individual participant workbooks containing all the exercises are available for this program. When the participants have completed all the activities and written assignments, they will have, for their future reference, a meaningful record of this period in their personal growth.

CHAPTER ONE

THE EFFECTS OF SELF-ESTEEM
A Boy Named Jamie

CONTENTS

LEADER'S INFORMATION
> Self-esteem
>
> Producing change
>
> Personal steps required for change
>
> Communication and conflict

INTRODUCTORY EXERCISE (Who Am I?)

CHAPTER SUMMARY

SIGNIFICANT POINTS AND OBJECTIVES

EXERCISE TOPICS
> Effects of early conditioning
>
> Self-esteem: What it is and how it affects us
>
> Low self-esteem: Causes and ways to improve it
>
> How to handle people who are hurtful

LEADER'S INFORMATION

SELF-ESTEEM

Low self-esteem is the core issue responsible for many of the problems that we see in youngsters today. Acting out and withdrawal, although they appear to be opposite behavioral extremes, are in fact often reactions related to how people feel about themselves. Those who experience problems related to low self-esteem often believe that no one else could or does feel the way they do. Feeling unique and alone, which adds to their discomfort, can cause some young people to: isolate themselves even more, seek out others they can feel a level of comfort with, or try to hide their feelings by creating an unreal image. This *Guide* has been developed to help all young people, especially those with low self-esteem, to better understand:

- the adolescent period and what it involves

- their own feelings and to realize that they are not alone

- there is hope for improving their situation

- they have options and choices available to them for improving their lives

PRODUCING CHANGE

To resolve or alter problems and concerns one must first recognize and accept that a problem exists. This can be a difficult first step, often engulfed in resistance and denial. A group or class activity is often helpful in breaking through the fears that cause this resistance. The process of relating to others with similar feelings works well in helping one to acknowledge their own situation. The next step involves accepting the fact that we all have the ability to produce change within ourselves. This is followed by the desire or motivation to produce such change. When the desire is strong enough, a personal commitment is made to do the work required to produce change. The following diagram represents the sequential steps involved in producing change.

PERSONAL STEPS REQUIRED TO PRODUCE CHANGE

- Recognize a problem exists (acceptance)
- Develop an understanding of the problem (awareness)
- Acknowledge ability to produce change (personal power)
- Become motivated to produce change (desire)
- Make a commitment to the process of change (choice)
- Do whatever is required to produce change (work)
- Maintain the desire to continue the process (persistence)

This *Guide* and its exercises will make it possible for teens to attain a greater awareness of the positive choices available to them. These choices will enhance their outlook for the future. With this renewal of hope comes the stimulation to reach for and realize one's true potential.

COMMUNICATION AND CONFLICT

Young people sometimes do not deal with conflict situations in a positive way. They may become extremely defensive by attacking or withdrawing. While an attacking behavior normally results in increased hostility and conflict, withdrawal leaves the problems unresolved, with the feelings of anger remaining. Explaining how one feels to the other person is the most satisfactory option. It is important to realize that talking about one's own feelings, as opposed to telling the other person what he or she is causing (blaming), is a response that is nonthreatening and stands a much better chance of being heard. The use of "I" statements instead of "YOU" statements is a constructive means of dealing with conflict resolution (I vs. YOU statements will be discussed at greater length in later chapters).

INTRODUCTORY EXERCISE
WHO AM I?

OBJECTIVE

To introduce the participants to this program by creating:
- a safe atmosphere for sharing the exercises that follow
- a preliminary awareness of the self

LEADER'S NOTES

The first part of this Teen Issues/Self-Esteem Program involves an exercise, Who Am I?, which will help introduce the participants to the program and to one another. The written portion of this exercise is followed by participant sharing and discussion, first in small groups, then in the whole group.

(A) Things I Like Best About Me focuses on the three positive qualities they like about themselves and why they like those qualities best.

(B) The Things I Like to Do Most requires them to list their three favorite activities; this could include something specific about work, school, fun, sports, etc. Examples: playing baseball, watching the TV program "Dallas," or going to the movies, etc. For each of these favorite activities, they are to add their reason why those are their favorites (why they chose them).

(C) My Favorite People requests the participants to list the three favorite people in their lives and the reasons for their choices. This should include people they have an involvement with, not rock or movie stars.

(D) What Would Make Me Happier? asks the question: If you were given one wish for something that would make you happier than you are today, what would you wish for and what are your reasons for choosing that wish?

(E) The One Thing I Like Best About Me requests the completion of the sentence: The one thing I like best about myself is _____. They are also asked to give the reason for their choice.

(F) To Help You Know Me asks for the one thing they would like to add in the form of description about themselves that would be helpful to others to better know them. This task is accomplished by completing the sentence: To describe myself best, so that others might know me better, I would like to add that I am_____.

* * * *

WHO AM I?

(Some Things to Share About Me)

(A) Things I Like Best About Me

List three positive qualities you like about yourself and why.
1.
Why?
2.
Why?
3.
Why?

(B) The Things I Like to Do Most

List three of your favorite activities and why you like them.
1.
Why?
2.
Why?
3.
Why?

(C) My Favorite People

List three of your favorite people, who they are (friend, family member, etc.) and why they are meaningful to you.
1.
Why?
2.
Why?
3.
Why?

Who Am I? (continued)

(D) What Would Make Me Happier?

List one wish that, if granted, would add something meaningful to your life and would make you happier. Explain why.
1.
Why?

(E) The One Thing I Like Best About Me

Finish the following sentence:
The one thing I like best about myself is:
Why?

(F) To Help You Know Me

To describe myself best so that others might know me better, I would like to add that I am:

*   *   *   *

CHAPTER SUMMARY

THE EFFECTS OF SELF-ESTEEM
A Boy Named Jamie

This chapter begins with Jamie English, a 42 year old adult, reflecting on his adolescent years, and the impact they have had on his development into adulthood. Throughout his story he relates his feelings and the events as they began that summer of his 12th year. Twelve-year-old Jamie introduces his parents, his older brother George who is away at college, and himself. Jamie questions every aspect of his life, including why he was named Jamie. In describing his unhappiness with his parents, he tells how he is often compared to and asked why he isn't more like his older brother. Because of how he feels about himself, Jamie chooses to spend much of his time alone. Jamie's idea of enjoying his summer vacation is staying alone in his room with his thoughts. His fears of the outside world are confirmed as he encounters Marty the local bully. Escaping from Marty and his hurtful remarks, Jamie goes to the only other place besides his home where he feels somewhat safe, an isolated area away from the other kids he calls his "private and secret place." Alone, Jamie questions why he needs to be so sad. When no one replies he asks, "Why can't anyone hear me?" While in this secret place, Jamie often falls asleep and sometimes has terrible dreams. He recalls one very scary dream. In this dream he is trapped in a large, clear cylinder with crowds of people staring in and laughing at him. For a long time after his frightening dream, Jamie resists falling asleep. This day proves to be different for Jamie. Alone and tired, he drifts into a deep sleep, only to be awakened and startled by a voice from behind him.

• Start each session with class/group inputs on what the chapter is about.

SIGNIFICANT POINTS, OBJECTIVES AND EXERCISES

POINT #1

Jamie English, the adult, looks back on his youth. He reflects on the feelings he had as a twelve-year-old and the impact that period had on his life.

Everything learned and experienced in one's youth affects adulthood. Whether those experiences and inputs have been positive or negative, they impact us by either providing good guidelines or handicaps to be overcome. Conditioning plays a significant role in determining what each person will be like and will become in the future. Each student should be made aware of the effect of positive and negative learning and that adverse conditioning can be overcome.

OBJECTIVE

To recognize:
- the effects of early conditioning
- that adverse conditioning can be overcome
- the importance of altering negative learning

LEADER'S NOTES

Exercise 1A: Ask the group to rate the four answers listed (using 1 through 4, with 1 being best and 4 being the least likely) as their response to the question: Why are some people able to overcome the difficulties of their youth, while others are not. Show their answers in a grid on the chalkboard. Follow up with a discussion of the rationale for their choices.

Exercise 1B calls for two well known historical figures to be listed, with a selection of two factors from the multiple-choice list of success factors that helped them become successful. Examples: Abraham Lincoln c, (highly motivated), d, (understood the value of education) and f, (connection with social needs); and for Martin Luther King, c, d, and f could apply.

Exercise 1C requests the same information as in Exercise 1B, only 1C applies to people they know. The same list of choices are available for the success factors.

Exercise 1D calls for a listing of the success factors the people in 1B and 1C have in common. The discussion that follows this exercise should involve an exploration of the importance of these common factors for overcoming the difficult times of one's youth and if these common factors may be a key to the success of all people.

EXERCISE #1
(A) Overcoming Difficulties of Youth
(B) Overcoming Negative Learning - Historical Figures
(C) Overcoming Negative Learning - People You know
(D) Common Success Factors

*   *   *   *

POINT #2

Twelve-year-old Jamie is an unhappy young man who is unable to enjoy his summer vacation.

Time weighs heavily on the unhappy person. For Jamie, summer vacation means facing his fear of other young people and the outside world. Although he tries to remain hidden in what he regards as the safety of his bedroom, his mother insists that he go outside and play.

OBJECTIVE

To understand:
- what self-esteem is
- the role self-esteem plays in how people behave and relate to others
- how feelings are reflected in dreams

LEADER'S NOTES

Exercise 2A requires a written response to the question: Jamie lived in his own world, which excluded others. Why did he dislike summer vacation?

Exercise 2B provides a list of twelve possible reasons why young people choose to remain alone. The participants are asked to select three reasons that feel right to them. They are also asked to number their reasons #1 through #3, with #1 being the most important.

After the completion of the written portions of Exercises 2A & 2B, ask for group responses. Record on your chalkboard the group results of 2B (the three major reasons why a young person would choose to exclude himself from others). The important points are to identify some self-esteem factors and to understand how self-esteem (how people feel about and view themselves) can affect their level of functioning.

For Exercise 2C, have the group write their definition of self-esteem. Through group discussion, develop a meaning for self-esteem which all the participants can accept and understand.

Exercise 2D, have the class discuss their thoughts on the meaning of Jamie's dream (being in a cylinder with people staring in at him). Defining what the dream means to them may evoke many different responses. It would be helpful for them to know that dreams often reflect the feelings people carry of themselves. This particular dream reflects Jamie's poor self-image and his fears of the outside world and the people in it. Those same fears keep Jamie from wanting to play outside.

EXERCISE #2
(A) Jamie Disliked Summer Vacation
(B) Jamie Chose to Remain Alone
(C) What Is Self-Esteem?
(D) What Did Jamie's Dream Mean?

*   *   *   *

POINT #3
Jamie chooses to spend his time alone, obviously not feeling too good about himself..

Low self-esteem (how we feel about and view ourselves), affects how we relate to others and most everything that we do in our lives. Many young people and adults suffer from feelings of low self-esteem.

OBJECTIVE
To understand:
- some of the causes of low self-esteem
- ways of improving low self-esteem

LEADER'S NOTES
Exercise 3A asks the participants to express their thoughts on what caused Jamie to view himself in such a negative way. The sharing of answers following the written exercise should include self-esteem as a cause for his actions.

Exercise 3B asks the participants to offer their opinions on what Jamie or someone like him could have done to feel better about himself and his situation. Upon the completion of the written exercise, the group will explore in small groups what young people can do to overcome those things that cause them to feel so bad about themselves. What the small groups come up with should be discussed by the whole group. Some examples might include: thinking about positives instead of negatives; communicating what's bothering them; seeking help from parents, school, church or friends.

EXERCISE #3

(A) Why Did Jamie View Himself in a Negative Way?

(B) What Could He Have Done to Feel Better?

* * * *

POINT #4

Jamie feels hurt when his parents compare him to his older brother. They ask him why he can't be more like his brother George.

Each human being is unique. To judge any person on a basis of making comparisons with anyone else can cause him or her to feel unloved and can adversely affect their self-esteem.

OBJECTIVE

To learn:

- how to handle people who have hurt you, while improving your relationship with them at the same time

LEADER'S NOTES

Exercise 4A uses true or false answers to help the group determine what Jamie did when his parents compared him to his brother. Follow up with group discussion on the responses to this question. Answers in sequential order: F, T, T, F, T, T, F, T, and F.

Exercise 4B asks the group to list options or choices that might have been available to Jamie for handling the situation in Exercise 4A and what the outcome might have been.

Exercise 4C asks which of the options from Exercise 4B might have brought about the best results for Jamie and why.

When the written portions of Exercises 4B and 4C have been completed, have your group break up into small groups to discuss their responses. Each group is to select a spokesperson who will take notes on what they agree upon. After the small groups return to the whole group, each spokesperson will share the three options they came up with, the one that would have been most helpful to Jamie, and their reasons. Allow for some follow-up discussion on what has been reported.

In Exercise 4D the same subject from Exercises 4A through 4C is continued as a role-playing activity. Have some group members volunteer to be Jamie or his parents. Jamie's parents' role would involve making comparisons between Jamie

25

and his brother George. Jamie's role would include applying what has been learned from Exercises 4A through 4C as a part of his responses and using "I" statements instead of "YOU" statements. Attention should be directed to how each role feels, and how different responses work for them. The leader should point out how to use "I" statements instead of "YOU" statements to communicate, without blaming, the feelings of being hurt. The whole group will then share their feelings about what they have learned. Direct the discussion to the importance of communicating the feelings of being hurt and how honest communication can help the relationship. Sometimes people aren't aware that what they are saying is hurting the other person.

EXERCISE #4

(A) How Jamie Reacted When Compared to His Brother

(B) Other Options and Choices

(C) Options and Their Results

(D) Role-Playing How Different Options Feel

* * * *

(A) Overcoming Difficulties of Youth

Jails are crowded with adults who have experienced difficult times in their youth, while others who have had the same upbringing, hold well-known positions in our society. Why are some people able to overcome the difficulties of their youth, while others are not? Listed below are possible causes for these differences. Use each of the four numbers only once, but use them all.

#1 = strong likelihood   #2 = possible   #3 = maybe   #4 = not likely

_____Wealthy family   _____High school graduate

_____Peer group   _____Good personality

What are the reasons for your order of selection?

(B) Overcoming Negative Learning
Historical Figures

List two historical figures (e.g., Abraham Lincoln, Martin Luther King, etc.) who experienced major difficulties in their youth and were able to overcome their early handicaps or conditioning to become successful. Select two success factors from the multiple-choice answers listed that you feel made it possible for these people to overcome the difficulties of their youth.

<u>Two Famous People</u>	
Name	**Success Factors** **(select from list below)**
1._____	_____
	_____
2._____	_____
	_____

Pick two of those listed below that provide the best reasons for that person's success.

        (a) inherited a fortune

        (b) had a mother who was a school teacher

        (c) highly motivated

        (d) understood the value of education

        (e) had a good support group

        (f) strongly connected with social needs

        (g) had high I.Q.

(C) Overcoming Negative Learning
People You Know

List two people you know who, like the famous people in Exercise 1B, experienced major difficulties in their youth and were able to overcome their early handicaps or conditioning. Select two success factors from the multiple-choice answers listed that you feel made it possible for these people to overcome the difficulties of their youth.

Two People You Know	
Name	**Success Factors** (Select from list below)
1._____	_____
	_____
2._____	_____
	_____

Pick two from those listed below that provide the best reasons for that person's success.

  (a) inherited a fortune
  (b) had a mother who was a school teacher
  (c) highly motivated
  (d) understood the value of education
  (e) had a good support group
  (f) strongly connected with social needs
  (g) had high I.Q.

(D) Common Success Factors

Compare the success factors that made it possible for the famous people in Exercise 1B to alter their early handicaps with those of the people you know in Exercise 1C. List those success factors they all have in common.

Common Success Factors
What success factors did the people in 1B and 1C have in common?

*   *   *   *

(A) Jamie Disliked Summer Vacation

Jamie lived in his own world, which excluded others. Why did he dislike summer vacation?

(B) Jamie Chose to Remain Alone

Here is a list of possible reasons why young people choose to remain alone and away from other kids. Select the three reasons that feel right to you. Number these reasons #1 through #3, with #1 being the most important and #3 the least important.

_____ Very bright
_____ Think they're better than others
_____ Kids make fun of them
_____ Think they're not attractive
_____ Poor personality
_____ Don't like people
_____ The youngest child
_____ Not very bright
_____ Don't like themselves
_____ Angry at their parents
_____ More important things to do
_____ Angry at themselves

(C) What Is Self-Esteem?

What does the term "self-esteem" mean to you?

(D) What Did Jamie's Dream Mean?

A group discussion exercise.

*   *   *   *

(A) Why Did Jamie View Himself in a Negative Way?

Based on what you have read so far, what do you think caused Jamie to view himself in such a negative way?

(B) What Could He Have Done to Feel Better?

What do you feel Jamie or someone like him could have done to feel better about himself and his situation?

* * * *

(A) How Jamie Reacted When Compared to His Brother

What did Jamie do when his parents compared him to his brother? Mark T for true or F for false next to each of the eight items below.

_____He told them he was angry.

_____He hid in his room.

_____He got angry at them but didn't tell him.

_____He joined the navy.

_____He sulked.

_____He thought less of himself.

_____He agreed with them.

_____He felt hurt.

_____He ignored what they said.

(B) Other Options and Choices

List three other options or choices that might have been available to Jamie for handling the situation in Exercise 1A. What do you think the outcome might have been?

Options:		
1.		
2.		
3.		
Outcome:		
1.		
2.		
3.		

(C) Options and Their Results

Which of the three options from (B) would have brought about the best results for Jamie? Why?	
Option#	Because

(D) Role Playing How Different Options Feel

Take turns role playing the above situation. Describe how you feel when you use a typical Jamie response or when "I" and "YOU" statements are used ("I" and "YOU" statements will be explained by your leader).

*   *   *   *

CHAPTER TWO

DEALING WITH REALITY
A Scary Dream

CONTENTS

CHAPTER SUMMARY

SIGNIFICANT POINTS AND OBJECTIVES

EXERCISE TOPICS
- Value of good friends
- Positive and negative character traits
- Importance of rules
- What to do about rules that seem unfair
- Listening and its value to communications
- Communication and its importance to the relationship

CHAPTER SUMMARY

DEALING WITH REALITY
A Scary Dream

Jamie's alone time is interrupted by a boy named Clarence. The two boys talk for a long time and find they have a lot in common. In spite of their initial discomfort, both being shy and introverted, they strike up an immediate friendship. Caught up in conversation with his new-found friend, Jamie overlooks the passing hours and his commitment to his parents to be home on time for dinner. He rushes home as quickly as he can, only to find his angry parents waiting for him. Sent to bed without dinner, Jamie falls asleep. He dreams of being a captive on a pirate ship commanded by "Marty the Terrible" (his real-life neighborhood bully). He is awakened by his mother, who brings him dinner and comforts him after his terrible dream. The two become more emotionally connected than ever before. His mother shows a willingness to listen to his feelings and concerns. As the summer passes, Jamie's friendship with Clarence grows deeper and he and his mother continue to feel closer. Jamie becomes aware that his parents argue more frequently. George, Jamie's brother, comes home for a visit from college. They enjoy their time together, but all too soon the family is saddened as George leaves to return to school. As the summer comes to an end, Jamie begins to feel anxious about leaving elementary school and entering junior high school in the fall.

• Before starting this chapter, review any questions the participants might have on issues covered in the previous session. This should be followed by group discussion of the current chapter.

SIGNIFICANT POINTS, OBJECTIVES AND EXERCISES

POINT #1

Jamie and Clarence become acquainted and realize how much they have in common. Through this meeting a strong friendship develops.

OBJECTIVE

To understand and recognize:
- the value of having good friends
- the qualities that good friends have
- positive and negative character traits

LEADER'S NOTES

Exercises 1A through 1D are written exercises which should be followed by a sharing of answers and discussion directed at gaining an understanding of the three parts of the objective for Exercise 1. The main point to be made from these exercises/group discussion is to increase awareness of positive and negative character traits and how they affect the way we react to others.

Exercise 1A asks the question: Jamie didn't have any friends until he met Clarence, why was Clarence's friendship so important to Jamie?

Exercise 1B asks the question: What three things attracted Jamie and Clarence to one another and helped them develop their friendship?

Exercise 1C requests the participants to: List two best friends and three things they like about each of their friends. (To assist with this exercise, you might ask the participants to think about why these two people are their best friends).

Exercise 1D is the opposite of 1C: Think about someone you know who you wouldn't want as your friend, and list three things about him/her you don't like.

EXERCISE #1

(A) Why Friends Are Important
(B) How Do People Select Friends
(C) Positive Qualities

* * * *

POINT #2

In enjoying his new friend, Jamie forgets his commitment to be home on time and is punished by being sent to bed without dinner.

OBJECTIVE

To understand:
- the need for living with and abiding by rules
- what one might do when he/she believes rules are unfair

LEADER'S NOTES

The following exercises pertain to the need for having rules to live by. Even though young people may view some rules as unfair, it is important for them to realize there are usually options available for negotiating or having unfair rules and laws revised. It must be stressed that living with rules and working to change those that seem unjust, is a more positive approach than breaking the laws that seem unfair.

In Exercise 2A, the group will mark each situational rule and its penalty as fair or unfair. They should also come up with three situations of their own having unfair rules and/or punishment.

In Exercise 2B, the group will state how they feel (fair or unfair) regarding Jamie being sent to bed without dinner and what they might do under similar circumstances.

In Exercise 2C, the group will select a situation from Exercise 2A they feel is unfair and offer their thoughts on how it might be changed.

Upon the conclusion of the three written exercises, the group should be lead in a discussion directed towards meeting the objectives of these exercises to understand the need for living with and abiding by rules and what people might do when they believe laws are unfair.

EXERCISE #2

(A) Who Needs Rules?
(B) You Be the Judge
(C) Choice Regarding Rules

*　　*　　*　　*

POINT #3

Jamie is awakened from his frightening dream by his mother. While comforting him, an important breakthrough takes place in their relationship as they make a connection with each other at a level they have not felt before. Jamie's mother does a lot of listening to his expression of feelings, and Jamie is elated by finally feeling heard.

OBJECTIVE

To recognize:

- what part listening and being heard play in being a good communicator
- the importance of communication to a good relationship

LEADERS NOTES

In Exercise 3A, the focus is on the importance of listening to good communications. This is accomplished through a role-playing activity. Through this activity, the group will feel discomfort and understand how frustrating it can be when they are not heard. They will also be made aware of how good it feels to communicate with an active listener (one who concentrates on what is being said, instead of what his/her own response will be). This subject, because of its importance, is expanded upon in Chapter 8, Exercise 2.

The main group is split into three role groups (see Role Playing Assignments which follows) for the purpose of providing instructions. Each of the three groups will be given different role assignments. Now have the whole group form into triads consisting of one role player from each of the three role groups. Allow approximately 10 minutes for this part of the role-playing exercise.

Role-Playing Assignments

#1 group

> The Number 1 role people will be told that their job is to communicate their disappointment with their best friend, who they just found out lied to them (the lie can concern any situation they want to create).

#2 group

> The role of the Number 2 people will be to interrupt any conversation going on within the triad with talk about their favorite interest or hobby (they will ignore anything that is said to them).

#3 group

> The Number 3 people will act interested in anything that is said to them and will remain responsive to whoever is talking to them.

41

Following the role-playing, each of the role types should be asked what it felt like to be ignored, interrupted, or listened to. The focus of the discussion that follows should be directed toward what they felt and the value of the listener to the communication process.

In Exercise 3B, the participants are asked to describe good communication skills and tell why good communication is important to a relationship. Value of good communications to the relationship is stressed.

EXERCISE #3
(A) So Who's Listening?
(B) What's in a Relationship?

* * * *

(A) Why Friends Are Important

Jamie didn't have any friends until he met Clarence. Why was Clarence's friendship so important to Jamie?

(B) How Do People Select Friends?

What three things attracted Jamie and Clarence to each another and helped them develop their friendship?

1.	
2.	
3.	

(C) Positive Qualities

List your two best friends and three things you like about each of them (why you chose them as friends).

	NAME	WHAT YOU LIKE ABOUT THEM
1.		(a)
		(b)
		(c)
2.		(a)
		(b)
		(c)

(D) Negative Qualities

Think about someone you know who you wouldn't want as your friend, and list three things about him/her that you don't like (do not list their names).

1.	
2.	
3.	

* * * *

(A) Who Needs Rules?

The following list contains examples of different situations in our society. Next to each situation is a rule and the penalty that applies when the rule is not obeyed. Are those situations affected in a positive or negative way by the rules that apply to them? Mark "F" for "fair" and "N" for "not fair" next to the rules. Use the same letters to mark the penalties that are fair or unfair.

WHO NEEDS RULES?		
Situations	**Rules**	**Penalty**
driving too fast	☐ established speed limit	☐ tickets/fines
shoplifting	☐ laws regarding stealing	☐ fines/jail
physical abuse	☐ laws regarding abuse	☐ fines/jail
late for dinner	☐ parents' rules	☐ punishment
not paying taxes	☐ government law	☐ fines/jail
ignoring dress codes	☐ school rule	☐ suspension
refusing military service	☐ government law	☐ jail
late to school	☐ school rules	☐ tardy notice
late to bed	☐ parents' rules	☐ punishment

Now add three situations that you think have unfair rules. Also include the rules and the penalties that apply to the situation.

Situation	Rules	Penalty
1.		
2.		
3.		

(B) You Be the Judge

Sometimes rules and their penalties or punishment seem unfair. How do you feel about Jamie's punishment when he came home late for dinner? Was it fair or unfair?

What choices, if any, did he have for dealing with what took place?

What might you have done in the same situation?

(C) Choice Regarding Rules

Which one situation in Exercise 2A seems most unfair to you? What might be done to change that rule?

* * * *

(A) So Who's Listening?

A role-playing exercise. (Instructions to be provided by leader)

(B) What's in a Relationship?

Describe good communication skills. Why is good communication important to a relationship?

*   *   *   *

CHAPTER THREE

ADJUSTING TO CHANGE
Scrubs and Junior High

CONTENTS

CHAPTER SUMMARY

SIGNIFICANT POINTS AND OBJECTIVES

EXERCISE TOPICS
    Reacting to new situations
    Rational and irrational fears
    Fear can control one's ability to function
    Behavior associated with insecurity

CHAPTER SUMMARY

ADJUSTING TO CHANGE
Scrubs And Junior High

Autumn begins and Jamie prepares as best he can for entering junior high. On the first day of school, he awakens feeling nervous and frightened as he anticipates what this new experience will be like. While waiting for the bus he observes other kids, including Marty, looking as scared as he. Jamie's fears grow stronger, adding to his feelings of confusion as he enters Farnsworth Junior High. While asking directions of some other students, he is made fun of and called "scrub." Jamie is rescued from these older students and their name-calling by the prettiest girl he's ever seen. She introduces herself as Diane. With her help, they arrive at the auditorium for the new-student orientation. As they go their separate ways, Jamie keeps thinking of Diane's beauty and how helpful she was to him. In his homeroom class Jamie attempts to feel more secure by taking a seat in the rear of room. He is shocked as Marty chooses the seat next to him. Jamie accepts Marty's suggestion that they have lunch together, thinking it might be less scary than eating alone on the first day. Jamie feels concerned about not seeing Clarence at school and wonders what might be wrong. At home, things aren't any better for Jamie, for his parents continue to argue. At night, to hide from the sound of their arguing and the pain he feels, Jamie buries his head in the pillow, wishing was all a bad dream.

• Before starting this chapter, review any questions the participants might have on issues covered in the previous session. This should be followed by group discussion of the current chapter.

SIGNIFICANT POINTS, OBJECTIVES AND EXERCISES

POINT #1

On Jamie's first day at Farnsworth Junior High he is extremely fearful of this new situation. However, Diane, also there for the first time, appears quite calm as she rescues Jamie from some other students.

OBJECTIVE

To understand:
- how people react differently to new situations
- the difference between rational and irrational fears
- how fear can control one's ability to function

LEADER'S NOTES

The main purpose of these exercises is to help teens understand that fear may cause some people to react differently to similar situations, some fears are realistic while others are not, and fears can affect one's ability to function.

This session provides the introduction to the subject of fear, which will be explored in greater depth in Chapter 11, "Breaking Out Of The Fear Cycle."

Exercise 1A asks for participant's thoughts on what caused Jamie and Diane to respond differently to their first day at school (Jamie, nervous, and Diane calm). Follow by discussion so the group can share their ideas.

Exercise 1B is a true-or-false activity directed at helping the group understand the difference between rational and irrational fears. The answers are: 1,3,7 and 9 are true and 2, 4, 5, 6, and 8 are false. The group results for Exercise 1B should be shown on the chalkboard as a catalyst for the discussion of rational vs. irrational fears. The discussion should help ensure that the terms rational and irrational, as they apply to fears, are understood.

In Exercise 1C, the group selects one fear from Exercise 1B that could affect the greatest loss of control over normal day-to-day functioning. They are also to add the reason for their selection. A number of answers could be correct. The important point for them to understand through the sharing that follows is that some irrational fears have a greater effect upon us when they control our ability to function. Obviously, being afraid of sharks isn't going to affect one's ability to function as much as being afraid of people would, unless that individual is a deep-sea fisherman or a shark trainer.

EXERCISE #1
(A) New Situations and Fear
(B) When Does It Make Sense to Be Fearful?
(C) When Fear Is the Boss

*   *   *   *

POINT #2
On their first day in junior high, Jamie is surprised by Marty acting frightened. Jamie has always viewed Marty as being so sure of himself and now he sees another side of him.

The behavior reflected by an insecure person may sometimes show itself as being opposite to how they feel. They may try to cover up how they truly feel about themselves by projecting another image.

OBJECTIVE
To recognize:
- the behaviors associated with insecurity
- how those feelings can reflect themselves in different behaviors
  Marty, extroverted and Jamie, introverted

LEADER'S NOTES
Marty and Jamie are good examples of how people may respond differently to their feelings of insecurity and low self-esteem. Exercise 2A involves matching those behaviors and feelings listed in the exercise with the story characters of Diane, Marty, Jamie and Clarence. Then identify those characters and their behaviors as having feelings of security or insecurity. The terms "security" and "insecurity" should be developed by the group or explained prior to the start of the exercise. (Security meaning feeling comfortable with oneself and what one is doing and insecurity being the opposite or feeling uncomfortable with oneself and one's activities).

The 2B portion of this exercise deals with the more personal side of this issue, as the group reports in journal format some of the reasons for their actions and behavior being opposite to the feelings they have. Based upon time available, the journal writing can be done at home. Anyone desiring to share his/her journal activity should be allowed to do so.

These exercises can be concluded with a group discussion on the results of Exercise 2A: the difference between feeling secure and insecure and why some people like Marty act one way when they're feeling another way.

EXERCISE #2
(A) What They Feel; What They Show
(B) What I Feel; What I Show

*   *   *   *

POINT #3
When Jamie hears his parents argue, he buries his head in his pillow.

Children often feel responsible when their parents have arguments. When the conflict continues, they may become fearful of losing their parents.

OBJECTIVE
To understand:
- how different people are affected by and react to conflict situations
  (Jamie hearing his parents arguing and feeling he caused it)

LEADER'S NOTES
Because this subject matter involves some highly sensitive issues, this "Personal Conflict Style" exercise will be used as a general exploration of the subject and its consequences.

In Exercise 3A the group will select responses that best fit their own reactions to various conflict situations and then select what they believe is a more appropriate behavior from the same group of responses. Upon the completion of this exercise the group should break up in triads for discussion of what they think the best answers might be for column (c) "The appropriate responses." The whole group should then discuss the results and the importance of handling conflict effectively.

EXERCISE #3
(A) My Personal Conflict Style

*   *   *   *

(A) New Situations and Fear

Jamie and Diane reacted differently to their first day at junior high. Describe what you feel was the main reason for Diane remaining calm and Jamie being so nervous on their first day in school.

(B) When Does It Make Sense to Be Fearful?

It makes sense to be fearful of some things we experience. We call those fears that make sense, rational. An example of a rational fear would be to be fearful of putting your hand on a hot stove because you know you would get burned. The opposite of rational fears are those that are irrational, or fears that don't make much sense. An example of an irrational fear or one that it doesn't make sense to be frightened of would be to be fearful of meeting someone new (as Jamie was).

Rational fear =	It makes sense to be frightened of it because there's a good chance you could be hurt. It warns you of danger.
Irrational fear =	That particular fear doesn't make much sense because there are no signs of danger.

For the situations below, write "T" for true and "F" for false.

1. _____ It makes sense to be fearful of touching something very hot.
2. _____ It doesn't make sense to be scared when jumping out of a plane with a parachute.
3. _____ It makes sense to be fearful of sharks.
4. _____ It doesn't make sense to be frightened of a loaded gun.
5. _____ It makes sense to be frightened of going to school when you know there have been fights at school.
6. _____ It makes sense to be fearful of tests you may fail at school.
7. _____ It doesn't make sense to be fearful of learning to drive a car.
8. _____ It makes sense to be frightened of people you don't know.
9. _____ It doesn't make sense to be frightened of the dark.

(C) When Fear Is the Boss

Jamie was so frightened of people that he didn't like going out of his house. When people stop their normal activities, like Jamie did because of his fear, it is said they are unable to function. It seems their fear has taken control. Which one fear listed in Exercise 1B would most likely affect one's ability to function? Why?

#	Reason:

*   *   *   *

(A) What They Feel; What They Show

Which character from the story best fits the behavior listed below? Use the first letter of the story's characters first names; M for Marty, D for Diane, C for Clarence, and J for Jamie. Next to each letter for a name, place an "I" for insecure or an "S" for secure, that you feel best applies to that person and his behavior. Although more than one character may apply to the behavior shown, use the one you think best fits.

Example:

_M-I_ angry	____frightened	____bright
____friendly	____shy	____assertive
____helpful	____aggressive	____nervous
____bully	____macho	____coward
____brave	____showoff	____happy
____sad	____leader	____follower
____honest	____actor	____dishonest
____foolish	____clown	____nice

Regarding their feelings of security and insecurity, what similarities were there between Marty and Jamie?

_____
_____
_____
_____
_____
_____
_____
_____
_____
_____
_____
_____

(B) What I Feel; What I Show

Marty acted as if he wasn't afraid of anything. We know from the story that he, like Jamie, was frightened of going into junior high. Marty tried to cover up his feelings by acting quite differently.

PERSONAL JOURNAL

This journal experience is quite personal and you do not need to reveal to the group what you've written. Its only purpose is to allow you to think about your own reasons for sometimes acting opposite to how you feel. Be sure to include as many details as you can think of to describe your feelings and experiences. You may begin by completing the sentence: I sometimes act differently than I feel because:

If required, use additional sheets of blank paper to continue your writing.

*　　*　　*　　*

(A) My Personal Conflict Style

Select those actions from the "RESPONSES" that best fit what you would do in the kind of situations described below. Place its number in the (a) column. After you have completed your reaction to all eight situations, select those actions you feel would be the best way to handle the same situations, and mark that number in column (b).

Example: Situation - Jamie hears his parents argue

Response - (a) bury my head in pillow

- (b) talk to parents

	What I would do (a)	Best way to handle (b)
SITUATION		
1. parent yells, didn't do homework	____	____
2. got blamed for something I didn't do	____	____
3. bully at school wants to start a fight	____	____
4. teacher yells at me for talking in class	____	____
5. friend lies to me	____	____
6. someone steals my lunch money	____	____
7. store doesn't take back scratched record	____	____
8. got thrown out of movie by manager	____	____

RESPONSES:

1. cry	9. seek help
2. ignore them	10. do the same thing to them
3. hit him/her	11. say I'm angry
4. explain	12. report them
5. get defensive	13. do nothing
6. run	14. get even
7. yell back	15. never deal with them again
8. say I'm sorry	16. write a letter

17. tell him/her I'm disappointed in his/her action

* * * *

CHAPTER FOUR

CAN YOU ESCAPE FROM LIFE?
Mystery Involving Clarence

CONTENTS

CHAPTER SUMMARY

SIGNIFICANT POINTS AND OBJECTIVES

EXERCISE TOPICS
    Feelings about suicide
    Other choices
    Denying or accepting reality
    Development of a personal emergency plan

CHAPTER SUMMARY

CAN YOU ESCAPE FROM LIFE?
Mystery involving Clarence

Jamie tries to reach Clarence, without success. Clarence's father calls Jamie and asks him to come over after school. After talking to Clarence's parents, Jamie is shocked to learn that Clarence tried to take his life by taking an overdose of sleeping pills. Clarence's parents ask Jamie if he might know what could have caused such a thing to happen. When Jamie goes home, he becomes more upset by his father saying that such a thing could not happen in their family. Jamie, upset over what is going on with his friend, feels something like that could happen to anyone, even him. During his first visit with Clarence they both feel uncomfortable, yet Jamie realizes they have a lot more in common than he had thought. Later, in the quiet of his "secret place," he tries to understand what caused the situation to take place and why Clarence hadn't talked to him about it first. At home, Jamie becomes more frightened by his parents' constant arguing. Feeling unworthy and unloved, Jamie continues to experience pain and confusion. He finds himself wishing he could escape from the pressure and run away from his life. Jamie suddenly realizes what Clarence might have been feeling. He becomes more frightened about the similarities in their situations and realizes that if Clarence could have spoken to his parents none of this might have happened. Jamie promises himself that before he ever gets to that point, he would speak to his parents or anyone else who would listen to him.

• Before starting this chapter, review any questions the participants might have on issues covered in the previous session. This should be followed by group discussion of the current chapter.

SIGNIFICANT POINTS, OBJECTIVES AND EXERCISES

POINT #1

Jamie finds out that Clarence has taken an overdose of sleeping pills.

The most serious form of withdrawal from the sometimes painful experiences of life and oneself is suicide. Approximately 400,000 teens attempt suicide each year, with 5,000 dying as a result of their action. Teenage suicide jumped 70% from 1960 to 1970 and another 40% between 1970 and 1980.

OBJECTIVE

To focus on:
- the feelings involved when someone you know has made an attempt at or has committed suicide
- any other factors that may contribute to this drastic action
- more positive choices

LEADER'S NOTES

Exercise 1A involves the participants developing their own thoughts about why Clarence, or someone like him, would take an overdose of pills. They are asked to select two factors from a list provided that they think are the most likely choices.

In Exercise 1B, individually the group will come up with three things they might say or do when someone they know is talking about taking his/her life. These thoughts will then be used as their initial responses for the brainstorming session in 1C.

Exercise 1C involves listing the responses from the group on the chalkboard. Then, through the process of selection (voting), agreement is developed for the best course of action when a friend indicates thoughts of suicide.

EXERCISE #1

(A) Why Did Clarence Do It
(B) What Do You Say or Do?
C) Brainstorm Choices and Options

* * * *

POINT #2

Jamie becomes quite angry when his father says that Clarence's situation could never happen in his family. The truth for Jamie is that it could happen. He realizes, by his father's comments, how little he understands how badly Jamie hurts at times.

OBJECTIVE

To understand:
- the difference between denial and acceptance of reality
- what effect the pattern of denial can have upon an individual

LEADER'S NOTES

Exercise 2A will allow the young people to think about why people sometimes have difficulty in accepting the truth and choose denial in its place. The group is asked to select two or more items from the list provided that they feel kept Clarence's parents and Jamie's father from accepting the truth. They are then asked to provide their thoughts on why their selections best fit he reasons Jamie's father and Clarence's parents had for denying the truth. There are no incorrect answers for the selection part of this exercise. The value to be gained from this exercise comes from the understanding gained from why some people use denial.

A group discussion should follow in which they share the factors they selected, their reasons, and the negative outcome of denying the truth of what's happening. Denial is a form of resistance. When one can accept the truth, as painful as it may be, then and only then can they produce change (philosophy of A.A. organization and one of the significant factors of psychotherapy).

Exercise 2B is a true-or-false activity in which the group explores the results of accepting or denying the truth. Discussion and sharing should follow this exercise with its focus being on understanding the positive results of accepting one's true feelings in a situation as well as the negative results of Denial. All of the answers are true.

EXERCISE #2

(A) Afraid to Accept the Truth
(B) Accepting What Is

*   *   *   *

POINT #3

Jamie promised himself that before he would ever consider doing what Clarence did, he would talk to his parents and if they didn't listen he'd find someone who would.

Although many adults avoid the subject of suicide for fear of putting those thoughts into a child's mind, the truth is that discussion can be helpful as opposed to being harmful. A young person in pain who does reveal these thoughts stands a better chance of being helped.

OBJECTIVE

To consider and develop:
- constructive alternatives to withdrawing from life
- an emergency plan

LEADER'S NOTES

Exercise 3A helps define the need for young people to take positive action when and if they ever feel overly depressed, by developing their own personal emergency plan. This plan calls for them to indicate who they might seek help from (adults and/or young friends): Also included is any other positive action they might take. To stress the importance of this plan to their own well-being, a mock contract is provided for them to sign.

EXERCISE #3

(A) Your Emergency Plan

* * * *

(A) Why Did Clarence Do It?

What do you think caused Clarence to O.D. on his mother's sleeping pills? Pick the two most likely reasons reasons from those listed below.

_____ He was angry at his parents.

_____ He was getting a bad report card.

_____ He was sad.

_____ He didn't like his name.

_____ He didn't enjoy living.

_____ He wanted to get his parents' attention.

_____ He wanted to escape from what he was feeling.

_____ He was afraid of going to junior high.

_____ He wanted people to feel sorry for him.

_____ He was feeling a lot of pressure.

(B) What Do You Say or Do?

Come up with three things you would say or do to help Clarence or someone like him who is talking about committing suicide.

1. _____

2. _____

3. _____

(C) Brainstorm Choices and Options

Group develops their best choices and options, using the inputs from Exercise 1B.

*　　*　　*　　*

(A) Afraid to Accept the Truth

Jamie's father said suicide couldn't happen in his family even though Jamie knew it could.

Clarence's parents kept calling what Clarence did an "accident." However, they knew it wasn't an accident.

Why were these people having such difficulty accepting the truth? Select at least two items from the list below that you think kept Clarence's parents and Jamie's father from accepting the truth. List your thoughts on why your selections best fit the reasons for these people being unwilling to face the truth.

1.____ They were afraid people would talk about it.
2.____ They felt it was their fault.
3.____ They were ashamed it happened (or could happen).
4.____ They were worried that it might happen again.
5.____ They didn't know how to talk about it.
6.____ They thought if they didn't talk about it, the problem would go away.

I selected No. ____ & ____ because:

(B) Accepting What Is

In Exercise 2A, you explored why some people are afraid to face the truth and learned about denial and acceptance. Now it's time for you to look at the results of accepting the truth of a situation as compared to denying the truth.

Answer the following true or false questions by indicating "T" for true or "F" for false:

1.____ Denying the truth in a painful situation makes less of a chance for changing or improving it.

2. ____ Acceptance of the truth is a first step towards making changes.

3. ____ If denial becomes a habit, some people may not know what the truth actually is.

4. ____ Denial and acceptance are opposites.

5. ____ Denial is negative because it is a form of lying to oneself.

6. ____ Acceptance is positive because it allows people to understand what they actually feel regarding their lives.

*   *   *   *

(A) Your Emergency Plan

Emergency plans are established to cover most potential disasters (fires, earthquakes, etc.). Jamie set up his emergency plan by promising himself that before he ever considered doing what Clarence did, he'd find someone who'd listen to him and then seek help by talking to that person.

What emergency plan do you have for yourself to cover those times when you are feeling that everything seems hopeless?

My personal emergency plan includes taking the following kind of action: Adults I would talk to:

_____

_____

Friends I would talk to:

_____

_____

Other positive things I might do:

_____

_____

_____

_____

A Contract with Myself

Because I believe that I am an important human being, I agree to take the best possible care of myself at all times. I realize that at times I may feel pressured and depressed. I also understand that these feelings don't last forever and that I will feel better. In signing this contract with myself, I agree that if there is ever a time when I'm feeling down and before I get to feeling too bad, I will put my emergency plan indicated above) into action.

_____

(signature)

* * * *

CHAPTER FIVE

BOYS AND GIRLS RELATING
Jamie's First Date

CONTENTS

CHAPTER SUMMARY

SIGNIFICANT POINTS AND OBJECTIVES

EXERCISE TOPICS
- How boys and girls relate
- Why people tease one another
- Why teasing affects some people
- Appropriate ways to get attention

CHAPTER SUMMARY

BOYS AND GIRLS RELATING
Jamie' s First Date

Jamie, after receiving an invitation from Diane to join her for lunch in the cafeteria, waits excitedly for his first date with a girl. While having lunch with him, Diane tells Jamie she has something very important to ask him. Jamie's fantasy is that Diane will ask him if he would like to go steady or something like that. Instead, her very important question concerns his opinion about how she will look in braces. Jamie's first date ends on a happy note with both Diane and him telling each other that they like one another a lot. Unable to concentrate on anything or anybody except Diane, including what is going on in class, Jamie receives an assignment on "Why It's Important to Pay Attention in Class." Clarence returns to school and shares with Jamie his reason for taking the pills. He tells him that his intentions were not to kill himself and that all he wanted to do was to get his parent's attention. Both Jamie and Clarence agree with what Clarence's therapist had said, "There are better ways to get attention than by hurting one's own self."

• Before starting this chapter, review any questions the participants might have on issues covered in the previous session. This should be followed by group discussion of the current chapter.

SIGNIFICANT POINTS, OBJECTIVES AND EXERCISES

POINT #1

Jamie was both excited and nervous about his date with Diane.

OBJECTIVE

To explore:
- attitudes and views about boys and girls relating

LEADER'S NOTES

Exercise 1 includes five questions covering boys and girls relating. Although this topic is of interest to young people, it will be a sensitive subject for group discussion. To make it easier for the participants to relate to and share, the exercise begins with a reference to Jamie's and Diane's first date in the cafeteria.

It is recommended that sharing be through small group discussion (triads) and conclude with inputs by the whole group. A recording of data from the small groups by an assigned recorder is helpful for tabulating the findings of the whole group and their discussion.

1. What may take place on a first date and what the determining factors are when dating begins. If age is the factor, then what age is the proper age to start? If age is not the determining factor, then what is?

2. Complete this sentence describing how you relate to the opposite sex: I am _____. Choose one of the following words which describes you best: aggressive, shy, assertive, reserved.

   Complete the following sentence: When around members of the opposite sex, I have a _____ time knowing what to say. Choose one of the following words which best fits your situation: difficult, easy, horrible, great.

3. What works best for you in starting a conversation with a member of the opposite sex and what subject is easiest to begin within that conversation?

4. What do you like least about members of the opposite sex?

5. What do you like best about members of the opposite sex?

EXERCISE #1

(A) About Dating

*   *   *   *

71

POINT #2

Marty teases Jamie about being in love with Diane.

OBJECTIVE

To explore:
- why people sometimes tease one another
- why some people are so easily affected by teasing

LEADER'S NOTES

This exercise, consisting of seven questions, adheres to the objectives shown above by having the group explore the act of teasing, why people tease, and why some people react to that teasing.. The questions should be followed by group discussion.

1. Describe the teasing that took place between Marty and Jamie in Chapter Five of the text.

2. Why did Marty act as he did regarding the teasing?

3. How did Jamie react to the teasing?

4. In your opinion, if a person like Jamie doesn't feel too good about himself (has low self-esteem), how might that affect how he reacts to people teasing him?

5. The group is asked to select the best-fitting answer from those provided to the question: Why do you believe you have been upset sometimes by people's teasing and not at other time? The participants are asked to give the reason for their selection. The best answer is (e), with (f) being an acceptable choice. Both answers deal with learning not to be affected by what someone else does. The (e) response is best because when one's self-esteem is high there is less chance of reacting to what other people say or do.

6. The participants are asked to answer the question, What could Jamie have done to handle his situation with Marty in a better way? In Chapter Eight they will become more aware that the best option for dealing with stress is to change their reaction to it.

7. Express the most important piece of learning for you regarding teasing and how to handle it.

EXERCISE #2

(A) Marty Teases Jamie

*   *   *   *

POINT #3

Clarence tells Jamie that his reason for taking the pills was to get his parents' attention.

OBJECTIVE

To explore:
- why some people choose negative actions (including self-abuse) to get attention
- appropriate actions for seeking help (which are more direct and produce more positive results)

LEADER'S NOTES

Exercise 3A covers inappropriate ways to get attention.

1. A list of actions and some accompanying feelings that people attempt to communicate through those actions are provided. The participants are asked to add three additional actions accompanied by the unspoken communications.

2. Multiple choice answers are used for determining what all of the actions and feelings have in common. The correct answer is (c) a desire to gain attention by inflicting something negative upon themselves.

3. Based on their knowledge of Jamie, Clarence, Marty and anyone else they know, they are asked: Why do some people use self-inflicting negative actions to gain attention? Discussion and shared information that follows will make the participants aware of the negative attention process that is used and why people practice this form of communication.

Exercise 3B Deals with better ways of communicating feelings and seeking help when it is needed.

1. The participants are asked to think of themselves as Clarence when he tried to gain his parents attention by taking an overdose of sleeping pills. For this activity they are asked to change his negative form of communication into a more positive approach.

2. Summarize what has been learned by answering three questions:

- What advice would you give to others and yourself if considering a negative action upon themselves/yourself to gain attention?

- What is the best way to communicate feelings?

- What is the most effective and appropriate way to get attention when you feel you need it?

The discussion that follows should ensure the group's understanding of what has been covered.

EXERCISE #3
(A) Getting Attention the Hard Way
(B) A Direct and Positive Method

* * * *

(A) About Dating

1. Jamie's first date with Diane involved their meeting in the school cafeteria. The best time for young people to start dating is something adults often question. In this activity we are interested in your views. The following questions will make it easier for you to explore your own thoughts and will then prepare you for small group discussions that follow.

Describe what you think takes place on a first date:

Do you feel age is the factor for determining when dating should begin? If so, at what age? If it isn't age, what would be the determining factor?

2. When it comes to relating with other young people of the opposite sex, which of the following words describes you best?

        I am _____.

      (aggressive, shy, assertive, reserved)

When around members of the opposite sex, I have a _____ time knowing what to say to them. Which of the following words best fits your situation?

      (difficult, easy, horrible, great)

3. What works best for you in starting a conversation with a member of the opposite sex? What subject is easiest for you to begin with?

4. What do you like least about members of the opposite sex?

5. What do you like best about members of the opposite sex?

*   *   *   *

(A) Marty Teases Jamie

After Marty found out Jamie and Diane were going to have lunch together, he teased Jamie about being in love with Diane. When people tease and make fun of one another, it is often quite painful. It is important to first understand why people create pain by teasing.

1. Describe in your own words how Marty teased Jamie (what did he say to Jamie?). You can refer to Chapter Five in your text.

2. With what you know about Marty's personality, why do you think he teased Jamie?

3. How did Jamie react to being teased by Marty?

4. In your opinion, if a person like Jamie doesn't feel too good about himself (has low self-esteem), how might that affect how he reacts to people teasing him?

5. Have you ever been in a situation where someone was teasing you and yet you weren't bothered by their teasing? Can you also remember another time and situation when you were hurt by someone else's teasing?

Why do you believe you have been upset sometimes by people's teasing and not at other times? Pick one of the following that feels best to you.

It depends on:

    (a) ☐ how good a teaser the person is

    (b) ☐ how I'm feeling physically

    (c) ☐ the weather

    (d) ☐ what my astrological signs say

    (e) ☐ how well I like myself at the time

    (f) ☐ how experienced I get in dealing with teasers

I made that choice because:

6. Sometimes people tease one another in a playful way with no intention of hurting the other person. But there are also times when insecure people work at tearing people down. They do this in a negative attempt at feeling better about themselves.

What could Jamie have done to handle his situation with Marty in a better way ?

7. What was the most important learning for you in this exercise on teasing and how to handle it?

*   *   *   *

(A) Getting Attention the Hard Way

1. In Chapter Five of the text, Clarence reveals to Jamie that his reason for taking the pills was to get his parents' attention. Some people do negative things to themselves to get attention from their parents, loved ones or friends. Many people do these things as a form of communication. The first column lists examples of actions taken to express feelings. The second column reveals the possible real message that person is trying to communicate without using words.

<u>Action</u>	<u>Communication</u>
I'm not going to eat dinner tonight	I'm angry at you
I'm not going to study for this test	I'm afraid I won't pass anyway
going against parents' advice	see how grown up I am
smoking	see what a big shot I am
fighting at school	I need to prove I'm tough
taking drugs	I'm not chicken and I want to be accepted

Add three more to the list (actions and communications) based on what you have seen people do.

_____   _____

_____   _____

_____   _____

2. All of the "actions" in the ACTION list of Exercise 3A - 1 have something in common. Select what you believe they have in common from the list below:

> They all show:
> (a) ☐ a willingness to take risks
> (b) ☐ that actions are easier to understand than words and are a more powerful form of communication
> (c) ☐ a desire to gain attention by inflicting something negative upon themselves
> (d) ☐ something natural that teens all go through as they experiment with growth
> (e) ☐ that parents don't understand teens

3. Why do some people choose negative actions to get attention? Think of Jamie, Clarence, Marty or anyone else you know of who has communicated in this way.

(B) A Direct and Positive Method

1. Hurtful actions against oneself or others is a <u>negative</u> form of communication (non-verbal). What would be a more <u>positive</u> and effective way to communicate the same type of situation?

Become Clarence for this activity. Clarence overdosed on pills to get his parents' attention through a non-verbal negative communication. Write what Clarence could have said to his parents that might have produced a positive outcome.

2. In closing this exercise, summarize what you have learned by answering the following questions:

What advice would you now give to others and yourself if considering a negative action upon themselves/yourself to gain attention?

What is the best way to communicate feelings?

What is the most effective and appropriate way to get attention when you feel you need it?

* * * *

CHAPTER SIX

DIVORCE AND GUILT
A Major Emotional Event

CONTENTS

CHAPTER SUMMARY

SIGNIFICANT POINTS AND OBJECTIVES

EXERCISE TOPICS
> Painful situations and accompanying guilt
> Stress can affect school and work activities
> Problems are not unique
> Feelings and thoughts

CHAPTER SUMMARY

DIVORCE AND GUILT
A Major Emotional Event

When alone, Jamie and Clarence share thoughts and plan their lives as adults. One day, Jamie is shocked by the news that his parents are going to separate. Believing himself to be the cause of their problems, Jamie feels guilty. Both he and his mother cry when his father gathers his belongings and leaves. Jamie visits his father at his new apartment and finds that he enjoys their time alone together. However, his feelings of guilt and sadness remain. Concerned about Jamie, Ms. Richards asks him to stay after school to discuss his falling grades. Unsuccessful in finding out what is causing his problems, she sends a note home asking for a conference with his parents. On the way home from school, Jamie and Marty talk about their situations at home, and Jamie finds he is able to relate to and feel sorry for Marty. He is shocked to find that Marty isn't as tough as everyone believes him to be. Jamie begins to see him as very much like Clarence and himself. When he arrives home, Jamie is surprised by his mother's reaction to the note he brings from school. Instead of being angry, she shows understanding and sympathy for what he is going through.

• Before starting this chapter, review any questions the participants might have on issues covered in the previous session. This should be followed by group discussion of the current chapter.

SIGNIFICANT POINTS, OBJECTIVES AND EXERCISES

POINT #1

When Jamie is informed by his parents that they are going to separate, he tells them that he knows he is the cause of their problems.

OBJECTIVE

To understand:

- how to deal with painful situations and the accompanying feelings of guilt (e.g. the divorce of one's parents)

LEADER'S NOTES

In Exercise 1A, a list of potentially painful situations are shown. The group will number the situations from 1 to 10, identifying #1 as the most painful and #10 as the least painful. They will also categorize each situation with an "X" under the four degrees of pain listed. When they have completed the sequential activity, lead the group in discussion on the reasons for their #1 selection and those selections they categorized as extreme. Also discuss why these situations are so painful, followed by what might be done to reduce prolonged pain (see list below.)

POSSIBLE ACTIONS

1. Write feelings in a journal or in a letter.

2. Talk to someone (have the group brainstorm to whom they might talk).

3. Avoid dealing with the situation (often used unsuccessfully, not considered a positive action for dealing with pain).

4. Become angry (a natural reaction as part of the grieving process).

5. Become involved in a (support) group where one can deal with problems and pain.

In Exercise 1B, the group will list three painful situations they have experienced, what eased the pain in those situations, followed by what they might do differently today based on the discussion in Exercise 1A. Exercise 1B should also be followed by discussion to review and reinforce what they have learned regarding the options available to them for dealing with pain.

Exercises 1C and 1D deal with feeling responsible and/or guilty for the behaviors of others.

In Exercise 1C, the group will list reasons why Jamie was or wasn't responsible for his parents separating.

In Exercise 1D, the participants will share whether they ever felt responsible or guilty for something that happened to someone else and how they got over their feelings. Upon the completion of the written exercise, the group should be led in a discussion related to their responses and feelings on the issue of Jamie's guilt and perhaps their own. Breaking the group into triads can be used and will work well as an introduction to the whole group interaction. It is important to get across the point that each individual is responsible for his/her own actions and not the actions or behavior of others.

EXERCISE #1
(A) Painful Situations
(B) My Own Experiences
(C) Jamie Felt Guilty
(D) Responsibility and Guilt

*   *   *   *

POINT #2
Jamie's grades drop from B's and C's to Failing. His behavior grades also take a nose dive, reflecting his reaction to what is happening within his family.

OBJECTIVE
To understand:
* how feelings and anger which produce stress can carry over from one's home situation and affect school and work performance
* how relaxing one's mind and body improves performance

LEADER'S NOTES

Exercise 2A demonstrates the effect that stressful situations can have upon one's school or work involvements. Remind your group of how Jamie's grades were affected by what was taking place at home between his parents. Have them participate by adding some of the facts from the story that speak to this incident, e.g. his father and mother arguing, his father packing his belongings and leaving, and Jamie feeling he caused it all.

As a part of Exercise 2A, instruct your group to close their eyes and think about some incident and/or individual that caused them to be upset and angry. When they clearly remember the situation and perhaps even visualize it, have them then open their eyes and in the space provided in their Workbook.,write about their feelings as they relate to that experience. Following the written portion of this exercise, determine through a show of hands how many participants got in touch with being angry or upset. Ask them to think about how upset they are and the situation that caused it, as they proceed with the next part of this exercise.

Without warning or preparation, begin Exercise 2B by telling the participants a test of their drawing and perception skills is required and they must try as hard as they can (term "try" produces stress) to draw a picture of an apple and write a paragraph describing the apple. Also tell them that this assignment will be handed in for grading. Inform them that they have five minutes to complete the exercise and no questions or talking will be permitted. When Exercise 2B is complete, have the group report on how they felt about the experience and then explain that this was not a test but that its purpose was for them to understand how stress can affect people.

Exercise 2C adds to understanding how stressful situations can adversely affect work and how relaxation can improve performance by showing the results of a relaxed approach to performing the same task. After explaining that this is not a test situation and that no papers need to be handed in, ask them once again to close their eyes. This time, suggest that they take some deep breaths and that with each breath they take, all stressful thoughts will leave them and will be replaced with deep relaxation. At this time, some peaceful music can help the relaxation process. However a soothing voice speaking about how good it feels to relax and that same voice counting backwards from 10 to 1 suggesting that with each number counted, they will feel more relaxed, will also help them to relax. After a few minutes, ask them to use their imagination (imagery) to see a large red apple. As you describe the apple to them, what it looks like, its stem, its size, its shape and its color, ask them to get in touch with what it feels like to be the apple, to even smell and taste it. Following a few minutes of this imagery and visualization, have the group redraw the apple as it feels to them and once again have them write their description of it.

LEADER'S NOTES (continued)

When they have completed this portion of the drawing and writing exercise, have the group compare their two drawings and descriptions for any apparent change or improvement. Request that they show and compare the two examples of their work with the group and share any feelings they have regarding the difference. As a closure to Exercise 2, the leader should summarize, explaining to the group how stressful situations within personal lives do carry over into our school work and how important it is to learn to deal with those stressors and use relaxation to improve how we feel and perform.

EXERCISE

(A) Stressful Incident
(B) A Fruitful Tale
(C) Relax and Enjoy It

*   *   *   *

POINT #3

Jamie is surprised when Marty shares information about the problems in his family and finds that he isn't the only one having problems of this sort.

OBJECTIVE

To understand:
- that many people share similar problems and feelings
- that sharing feelings and thoughts can be helpful

LEADER'S NOTES

Sharing feelings with a friend is something that most young people have experienced. However, when depressed, they often feel that what they are going through is unique and that no one else could feel so upset.

In Exercise 3A, the group will discuss the incident when Jamie and Marty shared similar problems and feelings related to what they were experiencing at home.

LEADER'S NOTES (continued)

Have two students read out loud, one taking Jamie's part and one being Marty. Start with the first paragraph on page 78 of the text and conclude the following sentence on page 80, "I wondered how he kept track of who he was, when he was so busy fooling everyone else." Begin the discussion by focusing on Marty and Jamie (the incident in the story) with the major focus being on Jamie feeling surprised that he and Marty shared similar experiences (that he is not the only one having parents who are separated or divorced) and realizing the benefits derived when feelings are shared.

EXERCISE #3
(A) Group Discussion

*　　*　　*　　*

(A) Painful Situations

When Jamie heard the news that his parents were going to separate, he experienced a lot of pain and he also felt guilty because he thought he had caused their problems. In this exercise various types of situations that can sometimes be painful are listed. Number these situations from 1 to 10. Number 1 will stand for the most painful situation and #10 will be the least painful. Next to each situation are types of pain: Extremely Painful, Moderately Painful, Slightly Painful and Not Painful. Choose the degree of pain for each situation and put "X" under the category that applies (extremely, moderately, slightly or not at all).

| | How it felt to you | | | |
| | Degree of pain | | | |
	Extreme	Moderate	Slight	None
__ Seeing a car accident				
__ Changing schools				
__ Losing a pet				
__ Failing a test				
__ Parents getting divorced				
__ Becoming ill				
__ Moving to a new city				
__ Seeing someone you care about involved in drugs or alcohol				
__ Being involved in a car accident				
__ Losing a parent				

(B) My Own Experiences

List three painful situations that have experienced and what you did to ease the pain.

Painful Situation	What Helped Ease the Pain
1.	
2.	
3.	

Based on what was discussed in Exercise 1A, what might you do differently to ease the pain if those situations were to happen today?

(C) Jamie Felt Guilty

Jamie blamed himself for having caused his parents to separate. Do you think he was responsible for what happened? _____Yes _____No
Give your reasons for your answer.

(D) Responsibility and Guilt

Have you ever felt responsible or guilty for something that happened to someone else even though you did not cause it to happen? How did you get over your guilt?

What took place?

```



```

How did you get over your feelings of guilt?

```



```

*   *   *   *

(A) Stressful Incident

You will be given information prior to working this exercise.

What are your feelings about it?

(B) A Fruitful Tale

You will be given information prior to working this exercise.

Descriptive paragraph

(C) Relax and Enjoy It

You will be given information prior to working this exercise.

Descriptive paragraph

*   *   *   *

CHAPTER SEVEN

DO PARENTS LOVE THEIR KIDS?
Another Side to Dad

CONTENTS

CHAPTER SUMMARY

SIGNIFICANT POINTS AND OBJECTIVES

EXERCISE TOPICS
    Value of sharing feelings
    Personal strengths and weaknesses
    Meaning of love
    When counseling is appropriate
    Making changes

CHAPTER SUMMARY

DO PARENTS LOVE THEIR KIDS?
Another Side to Dad

Following their meeting with Ms. Richards, Jamie's parents wait for Jamie to return from school. As Jamie enters the house and sees his parents, his expectations and thoughts turn to the punishment he will receive. Instead, he is pleasantly surprised when his father takes him in his arms and holds him close. Through the interaction that takes place, Jamie better understands what love is, and best of all, that his dad does love him. His parents, after sharing what has taken place in their meeting with Ms. Richards, reveal that she has recommended that Jamie see a counselor. They add that they too think it would be good for him to be able to talk with someone about whatever is bothering him. In answer to Jamie's questioning, his father explains why he feels differently now than he had in the past about counseling. He tells Jamie that much of his prior negative feelings were due to his own fear of looking more deeply into himself. Jamie's father reveals that he too is now seeing a counselor and getting much value from the experience. That evening, after accepting what has been proposed to him, Jamie prepares himself as best he can for entering into this new adventure. As he lies in bed, staring out the window at his favorite big oak tree, he becomes aware from the cold breezes blowing that another season has passed and winter has arrived.

• Before starting this chapter, review any questions the participants might have on issues covered in the previous session. This should be followed by group discussion of the current chapter.

SIGNIFICANT POINTS, OBJECTIVES AND EXERCISES

POINT #1

His father holds him close and Jamie knows what love is all about, and more importantly knows that his dad loves him.

There are times when young people question if their parents love them. It is important for them to know through actions and words that they do.

OBJECTIVE

To understand:
- the value of sharing feelings with people you care about
- what happens when caring feelings are not shared

LEADER'S NOTES

In Exercise 1A, the students will select their best answers in order of significance to the question, Why it is important to share feelings of love with family members? When they complete their selection, they will provide reasons for their top two selections. The seven possible answers listed in this Guide should then be listed on the chalkboard. Record the students' first and second choices and discuss them, followed with discussion on why they feel their choices are most applicable.

Exercise 1B allows the group to consider the same subject (sharing feelings of love) from Jamie's perspective, regarding how he felt about not knowing if his father loved him and what might he have done to find out. Group discussion should follow this exercise.

EXERCISE #1
(A) Sharing Loving Feelings
(B) When Love Is in Question

*   *   *   *

POINT #2

Jamie sees his tough old dad who hardly ever shows emotions crying, and he knows that no matter what follows, their experience of closeness will never be forgotten.

The belief that strength, especially in a man, is reflected by the absence of emotions and feelings is a myth reinforced by conditioning.

OBJECTIVE

To explore
- the meaning of love
- personal strength and weakness

LEADER'S NOTES

In Exercise 2A, your group will have the opportunity to explore the meaning of love and its importance. The discussion that follows can focus on their answers to the questions:

1. How do people know they are loved?

2. Why is love so important?

3. Why are positive feelings sometimes difficult to express?

4. What is love?

5. What is the opposite of love?

The last question (What is the opposite of love?) often gets the same response from children and adults: hate." Apathy is truly the opposite of love because love and hate are both high-energy involvements, whereas apathy lacks energy and caring. There is value in the group understanding how destructive apathy can be to any relationship or involvement.

Exercise 2B asks the participants to mark True or False as it applies to the eight statements provided on strength and weakness. The only true answer would apply to #4, "Expressing feelings is a sign of strength," all others would be false. The discussion regarding the question of strength and weakness may reflect both the cultural and societal values that both young people and adults carry which, unfortunately in many cases, carries the Rambo type of thinking and conditioning. Without needing to persuade those who may carry strong feelings on this issue, there can be value in just exploring different views and attitudes. From a psychological position, it is certainly healthier and emotionally strengthening to be in touch with and properly expressing one's feelings. It is a sign of weakness when one individual tries to control another.

EXERCISE #2

(A) What Is Love?

(B) Strength and Weakness

*   *   *   *

POINT #3

Acting on Ms. Richards' recommendation, Jamie's father explains to Jamie why he thinks going to a counselor would be a good idea for Jamie. Based on his parent's input and what Clarence has told him about how well he was doing in counseling, Jamie agrees to enter into counseling.

Counseling is most effective when accepted by the person who will be involved. When someone is forced into counseling they often bring a high level of resistance with them.

OBJECTIVE

To explore:
  • when counseling is appropriate and helpful
  • what to expect from the counseling experience

LEADER'S NOTES

Exercise 3A consists of personal journal experiences regarding possible issues the participants would want to talk about in counseling and what value they might gain from them. It should not be required to be shared with the whole group except for seeking their inputs and thoughts as it relates to the value of Jamie going into counseling. I recommend you mention that anyone wanting to discuss or share any part of their personal experience with you may do so in private.

EXERCISE #3

(A) The Counseling Experience

*   *   *   *

POINT #4

As a part of his explanation of why he changed his opinion about counseling and counselors, Jamie's father tells him about his own fears of sharing information about himself with others and of needing to look more deeply into his own life. He also indicates to Jamie that most people are fearful of change and therefore resist it whenever they can.

OBJECTIVE

To explore:
- why making changes in one's life is sometimes frightening
- why making changes is important to everyone

LEADER'S NOTES

Exercise 4A begins with the group exploring the following two questions:

1. Why was Jamie's father fearful of making changes in his life?
2. Why is it important for one to make changes?

Group participation should follow the completion of the written assignment. Answers might coincide with the following thoughts:

(a) Change in itself can be frightening to many people because it involves taking risks and doing something other than what falls into our normal pattern of living (our comfort zone).

(b) Change, as scary as it might be, is necessary if one is to improve oneself or to grow. If one does not change or grow, one becomes stagnant.

EXERCISE #4

(A) Making Changes

* * * *

(A) Sharing Loving Feelings

In this chapter, Jamie feels he understands the meaning of love and more importantly that his dad loves him. Jamie was not certain before that his father loved him

<u>Why do you feel it is important to share feelings of love with your family members?</u>

In providing your answer to this question, number the following possible answers from 1 to 7; #1 is the answer you like best and #7 the one you like least.

_____ so that people will like you

_____ because love is less stressful than hate

_____ to communicate how you feel

_____ so that you will feel better

_____ to improve your relationship

_____ to be honest with yourself and others

_____ because it's healthy to release feelings

Why do you feel your first and second answers are best?

#1 answer:
#2 answer:

(B) When Love Is in Question

How did Jamie feel about not knowing if his father loved him?

What might he have done to find out how his dad felt about him?

* * * *

(A) What Is Love?

Write a brief answer to the following questions about love. A discussion about what love is will follow.

1. How do people know they are loved?

2. Why is love so important?

3. Why are positive feelings sometimes difficult to express?

4. What is love?

5. What is the opposite of love?

(B) Strength and Weakness

In our society, the personal traits of strength and weakness are sometimes confused. As an example, Jamie's father at first hardly ever showed his feelings because he thought if men showed their emotions, they were weak. Identify which of the following statements you believe to be true and which are false. Use "T" for true and "F" for false.

☐ 1. Expression of feelings is strictly a feminine trait.

☐ 2. When men cry, they lose their strength.

☐ 3. Anger is a masculine trait.

☐ 4. Expressing feelings is a sign of strength.

☐ 5. Family members should understand how one another feels, without love needing to be said.

☐ 6. Emotional strength is related to being tough.

☐ 7. To take control over someone else is a sign of strength.

☐ 8. Emotionally, men are strong and women are weak.

*   *   *   *

(A) The Counseling Experience

This written journal exercise is personal and does not need to be shared with anyone. Its purpose is to have you explore what value you might see for yourself in being in counseling.

<u>PERSONAL JOURNAL</u>

If you chose to go to a counselor like Jamie did, what issues would you want to talk about?

What value do you feel you might gain from the counseling experience?

*   *   *   *

(A) Making Changes

Jamie's father spoke about how at one time he was frightened about making changes in his life. Why do you think he and others are fearful of changing?

_____
_____
_____
_____
_____
_____
_____
_____

Why is it important to make changes in one's life?

_____
_____
_____
_____
_____
_____
_____
_____
_____
_____
_____

*   *   *   *

CHAPTER EIGHT

THE COUNSELING EXPERIENCE
Sharing Secret Feelings and Thoughts

CONTENTS

CHAPTER SUMMARY

SIGNIFICANT POINTS AND OBJECTIVES

EXERCISE TOPICS
    Warning signs of stress
    Options for dealing with stress
    Communication; the importance of listening
    Value of trust
    Being overly responsible
    Feeling sorry for oneself ("poor me" attitude)
    The effects of self-improvement and self-concept

CHAPTER SUMMARY

THE COUNSELING EXPERIENCE
Sharing Secret Feelings and Thoughts

With the arrival of the winter season, Jamie begins his counseling experience. After getting past his initial meeting with his counselor Dr. Gerald Balding, his nervousness passes. Jamie finds that he enjoys sharing feelings and thoughts with someone who cares about him. Some of the issues Jamie deals with in counseling involve his desire to be closer with his father, how to be a better communicator, and finding that it's okay to have feelings. Jamie realizes, with Dr. Balding's help, that he isn't to blame for what his parents have been going through. Jamie's new learning helps him to begin viewing his life with more hope. As he becomes more hopeful, the darkness and confusion that was with him before begins to fade. As Jamie continues to work on those parts of his life that have caused him difficulty, other changes also begin to take place, and a new Jamie begins to emerge. As he senses these new changes within himself, Jamie finds himself liking the person he is.

• Before starting this chapter, review any questions the participants might have on issues covered in the previous session. This should be followed by group discussion of the current chapter.

SIGNIFICANT POINTS, OBJECTIVES AND EXERCISES

POINT #1

Jamie, extremely nervous about the new experience (counseling) he is about to enter into, perspires heavily as if it were mid-summer. After getting acquainted with Dr. Balding, Jamie feels more comfortable. By the end of their first session, he finds himself looking forward to future sessions

OBJECTIVE

To understand:
- the warning signs of stress
- how to relieve the feelings of discomfort and stress
- options for dealing with stress

LEADER'S NOTES

Exercise 1A consists of six questions dealing with stress and how to relieve it. Follow each one with group sharing and discussion.

1. The group learns what the warning signs of stress are and how their bodies react to stress.

2. The participants relate their own stress warning signs to events (situations or people).

3. The group is asked to explain what, if anything, they do to handle their stress. The discussion that follows should utilize the brainstorming process to produce positive methods for reducing the impact of stress and tension. Allow ideas to be presented without analyzing or questioning their validity and listing them all on the chalkboard for later review of what works best. Some inputs may include: distracting oneself through music, sports, reading,, talking to someone supportive, learning deep relaxation (using self-hypnosis, meditation, listening to a relaxation tape, etc.

4. The question is asked, Have you ever been in a difficult situation and someone did or said something that made you feel better? The importance of receiving and being supportive to the person experiencing stress should be mentioned. Counseling is often helpful to one under severe stress.

5. The participants are asked if they ever helped someone who was nervous and upset to feel better. What did they do and did it make a change in how they were feeling?

115

6. The group is asked to select the best option of the three listed options for dealing with stress (change their reaction to it is the most effective). They are then asked the reasons for having selected that option. The following provides information on the available options.

OPTIONS FOR DEALING WITH STRESS

(A) <u>Avoid stressful situation:</u> Stress is everywhere.To run from it without dealing with it may put you into another stressful situation, i.e. working on a job, your boss may put pressure on you; quitting the job to "avoid" the stress is a temporary fix, for you may very well come across another boss on the new job who will do the same to you or worse.

(B) <u>Change the situation:</u> When other people are producing pressure or stress that affects you, it is important for you to understand that you do not have the ability to change them or anyone else other than yourself. The boss, the teacher, the husband/wife, brother, sister or friend you may feel is adding stress to your life will only change when they decide to do so.

(C) <u>Change your reaction to the situation:</u> This is the most viable option. For the most part, you will not be able to successfully run from pressure situations and you are not able to change how other people act; you are able to take control of how you react to people and events producing stress. Although this behavior doesn't come easily for many people, it can be learned and is effective.

EXERCISE #1
(A) How Do You Feel When Stressed?

*   *   *   *

POINT #2
Jamie learns a lot from Dr. Balding about how people sometimes get their communication messed up. He also learns that communicating doesn't only mean speaking but that it also includes being a good listener.

OBJECTIVE
To learn:
- the value of good communications
- the part that listening plays in being a good communicator

LEADER'S NOTES

Chapter 2 Exercise 3, covered some initial work in the area of listening and communications. Because of its importance, this material is covered once again and expanded upon in this exercise (using different exercises to emphasize the subject).

Exercise 2A contains a self-assessment questionnaire in two parts. The first part includes many of the negative traits of poor communication and the second part, many of the positives to be found in the good communicator. The participants are asked to rate themselves on their communication abilities by marking statements: "N" for never or hardly ever does, "S" for sometimes, and "A" for always or most of the time. At the end of each of the two self-assessment sections, the participants total up their individual scores and compare them against the total group averages which are compiled on the chalkboard. It would be helpful to include group discussion on the positive and negative traits and what might be done to modify and convert the negatives into positives.

Exercise 2B begins with the group exploring the difference between the words "hear" and "listen" by looking up dictionary definitions and comparing them. This is followed by stating their feelings whether hearing or listening is harder to do.

Exercise 2C asks the group to rate how well some of the significant people in their life "listen" to them and to think about how these same people might rate the participant's ability to "listen." This activity continues as the group explores and writes their response to the question; What role does listening play in good communication and in developing sound relationships? This exercise concludes with their shared response to that question and a discussion on the significance of listening to communication and the correlation of how people feel about one another and how well they communicate.

EXERCISE #2

(A) Communication Self-Assessment
(B) What's the Difference?
(C) Rating Listeners

*　　*　　*　　*

117

POINT #3

Jamie's trust in Dr. Balding makes it easier to share his feelings with the doctor.

OBJECTIVE

To understand:
- the importance of trust in a relationship
- how to develop trust

LEADER'S NOTES

Exercise 3A contains seven questions that can either be worked in class or assigned as homework. The exercise focuses on trust, and the questions are to be answered individually in writing. In either case, the questions and answers should be used to provide the focus for group sharing and discussion directed at: what trust is and how important it is to good communication and healthy relationships.

EXERCISE #3

(A) Some Questions on Trust

*   *   *   *

POINT #4

Jamie tells the doctor how badly he feels, having caused his parents to argue and his father to move out.

OBJECTIVE

To learn:
- about being overly responsible for the feelings of others
- the effect being overly responsible for the feelings of others can have on all concerned

LEADER'S NOTES

Exercise 4A consists of four questions which can be assigned as homework or done in group. This exercise deals with learning to be responsible for one's own feelings instead of being responsible for the feelings of others. The questions and issues covered are:

1. Do you believe Jamie was responsible for his parents' arguments and for his father moving out?
2. Two statements are provided. A selection is required for the one they agree with and why this choice is more correct. Statements: (a) We must be willing

LEADER'S NOTES (continued)

to assume full responsibility for the happiness and well-being of someone we love (like a parent); (b) Although it is important to be caring and supportive of those we love, we must realize their feelings and actions belong to them. It is best not to assume responsibility for those things that are beyond our control.

3. What is the difference between being a responsible person and being responsible for others?

    Answer: In general, being a responsible person means being responsible for oneself and one's own actions.,whereas, being responsible for others, except in the case of infants and children, is beyond one's control.

4. Have you ever felt that you were the cause of your family's arguments? How did this make you feel?

    Guilt feelings often result when one assumes responsibility for the actions, behaviors and feelings of others.

Discuss the answers in triads first and then summarize the responses with the whole group. It is important that they understand the difference between being responsible for oneself, which is a positive quality and being overly responsible for others, which is a negative quality (often leads to attempting to control others). It is also important that the group understand how feeling guilty (like Jamie did) usually occurs when one feels responsible for another's feelings.

EXERCISE #4

(A) Assuming Responsibility for Others

* * * *

POINT #5

Dr. Balding explains how people use experiences, some of which are painful, to learn from and to bring about positive changes in their lives. He tells Jamie that while some people use these painful experiences to move forward and to become stronger, others continue to live with their negative feelings.

OBJECTIVE

To become aware of:

- the reason why some people choose to remain in a "poor me" place
- how choices affect the direction one takes in life

LEADER'S NOTES

Exercise 5A contains four questions dealing with personal choices:

1. Based on Dr. Balding's explanation in the text to Jamie, explain a "poor me "attitude.

2. Why do you suppose some people choose to remain in a "poor me" place feeling sorry for themselves? What do they get out of remaining in that place (what's their payoff)?

3. Have you ever felt sorry for yourself and then decided to do something about changing how you felt? What did you do to make the change?

4. The choices that you make affect the direction you go in your life. Explain what positive choices you might have made if you had been in Jamie's situation (experiencing emotional pain and feeling sorry for himself).

The important points to get across through discussion are:

- For some people the payoff or rewards for remaining in a "poor me" place is the sympathy they seek and often get. Another payoff might be seeking attention through the sympathy of others.

- Most important is the fact that as individuals, we have the power to make choices regarding how we react to the negatives in our lives and to either use them as learning tools in a positive way or otherwise.

- These choices affect the direction we go in our lives. There is an example that relates to this point in Chapter Sixteen of the text. Jeff Keith, a young man of 22 lost one of his legs to cancer and made the "choice" to run across the nation, raising funds for cancer research and providing hope for others with the disease.

EXERCISE #5

(A) Poor Me

* * * *

POINT #6

As Jamie works on improving himself, for the first time he begins to like the person he is.

OBJECTIVE

To explore:
- the value to be gained from self-improvement
- how improving one's self-concept can change one's life

LEADER'S NOTES

Because this is a lengthy chapter, we classify this exercise as optional, depending on availability of time and your group's ability. The activities involve written exercises followed by group sharing and discussion.

The focus and purpose of Exercise 6 is for the group to better understand the value of improving themselves and the meaning of self-concept.

Exercise 6A indicates that as Jamie made changes and improvements in himself, for the first time he liked the person he was. The participants are asked to explore any positive changes they have made in themselves and how good they felt afterwards. For example: improving how they looked or their school grades, etc. They are then asked to describe the event or change and how they felt afterwards.

Exercise 6B explains how, when personal positive changes are made, other good things happen. Jamie, after making improvements in his life, began to like himself and his whole life changed for the better. How people view themselves (like themselves) is called self-concept. Through this exercise, the group is asked to think about and describe some particular event that improved their self-concept and the effect it had on their life.

Exercise 6C asks the participants to:
- (a) provide their definition of the term "self-concept"
- (b) describe what Jamie, Clarence, Marty and Diane's self-concepts were during their early years
- (c) describe what their own self concepts are now

EXERCISE #6

(A) How Good It Feels
(B) I Like Me and the World Is Beautiful
(C) Evaluating Self-Concepts

*   *   *   *

(A) How Do You Feel When Stressed?

Jamie was extremely nervous about going into counseling. He perspired heavily when he came to his first session with Dr. Balding. However, by the time his meeting with the doctor was over, he felt so good that he was looking forward to coming back.

The discomfort Jamie felt (he perspired heavily even though it was wintertime) was his body's way of telling him he was in a stressful situation. In the following exercise, you will be able to explore how your body lets you know when you are experiencing stress.

1. How do you feel when you are in a tense or stressful situation? Check all of the items listed that you experience.

☐	upset stomach	☐	chills
☐	pounding heart	☐	tension in neck or back
☐	blush	☐	sweat
☐	tremble	☐	grit teeth
☐	dry mouth	☐	can't concentrate
☐	shortness of breath	☐	feeling upset or nervous
☐	nauseated	☐	headaches

Any experiences which are not listed (describe them)

☐ _____   ☐ _____

2. Do these stress warning signs take place when you are doing anything in particular or when you are with certain people? If so, describe when this discomfort most often seems to occur.

3. Explain how you handle the stress you're experiencing and the feelings that go with it. If you usually take no action, write what you feel you could do in the future that might help you.

4. Have you ever been in a difficult situation and someone did or said something that made you feel better? Explain:

5. Have you ever helped someone who was nervous and upset to feel better? What did you do? Did it make a change in how they felt?

I helped them by:

6. The three major options for dealing with stress are: (a) avoid the stress, (b) change the situation that produces the stress, or (c) change your reaction to the stressful situation. One of these three options is the best and most effective choice. Which one do you think it is? Why?

Which option is best?
Why?

*   *   *   *

(A) Communication Self-Assessment

In Chapter 2 Exercise 3, you worked on some exercises that covered the importance of listening to good communications. Because communication is the basis of all relationships, we will again cover the subject of listening and communicating, using a different type of exercise.

Jamie learned from Dr. Balding how people sometimes get their communication messed up. To get your thoughts and feelings across to others and theirs to you, is the basis for developing meaningful friendships and relationships.

To better understand how you communicate, and to improve your skills in this area of your life, you are to complete the following self-assessment questionnaires. The first questionnaire deals with negative communication traits and the second positive communication traits.

The questionnaires are shown on the following two pages

1. Negative communication traits

   Check one of the three boxes that feels right to you.

   N = never/hardly ever   S = sometimes   A = always/most of the time

   <u>N</u>   <u>S</u>   <u>A</u>

   ☐ ☐ ☐ monopolize the conversation
   ☐ ☐ ☐ interrupt
   ☐ ☐ ☐ make nasty comments
   ☐ ☐ ☐ put others down
   ☐ ☐ ☐ insult or verbally abuse others
   ☐ ☐ ☐ don't respect others' opinions
   ☐ ☐ ☐ demand your own way
   ☐ ☐ ☐ lose temper often
   ☐ ☐ ☐ tell lies
   ☐ ☐ ☐ answer questions with questions
   ☐ ☐ ☐ disagree a lot
   ☐ ☐ ☐ fail to keep promises
   ☐ ☐ ☐ make jokes when others are serious
   ☐ ☐ ☐ bragging, showing off
   ☐ ☐ ☐ thinking of what to say instead of listening to what

   ☐ ☐ ☐ COLUMN TOTALS (N's, S's and A's listed)

2. Positive communication traits

Check one of the three boxes that feels right to you.

N = never/hardly ever   S = sometimes   A = always/most of the time

<u>N</u> <u>S</u> <u>A</u>

☐ ☐ ☐ give others a chance to talk

☐ ☐ ☐ listen, even when you disagree

☐ ☐ ☐ greet others with a smile

☐ ☐ ☐ praise and compliment others

☐ ☐ ☐ willing to compromise

☐ ☐ ☐ treat others as equals

☐ ☐ ☐ be honest with others

☐ ☐ ☐ keep an open mind to what is being said

☐ ☐ ☐ can be trusted with information

☐ ☐ ☐ doing what you say you will do

☐ ☐ ☐ usually in a good humor

☐ ☐ ☐ express genuine interest in others

☐ ☐ ☐ treat people as you would want to be treated

☐ ☐ ☐ when in a conversation, look directly at the person

☐ ☐ ☐ trust others to be truthful until proven otherwise

☐ ☐ ☐ COLUMN TOTALS (N's, S's and A's listed)

(B) What's the Difference?

Jamie found out that listening is an important part of communication. Look up the words "listen" and "hear" in the dictionary and write their meanings as they apply to communicating.

Listen:

Hear:

What is the difference?

Which one is harder to do and why ?

(C) Rating Listeners

Rate how well the following people listen to you.

	never	sometimes	often	always
mother	☐	☐	☐	☐
father	☐	☐	☐	☐
brother	☐	☐	☐	☐
sister	☐	☐	☐	☐
best friend	☐	☐	☐	☐
teacher	☐	☐	☐	☐
boss	☐	☐	☐	☐

Now look at the relationship between how you feel about and get along with these people and how well they listen to you. Do you find that you feel better about those people that you rated in the "often" and "always" columns than those who fall into the "never" and "sometimes" column?

Yes _____ No _____

If those people who you just rated were to evaluate how well you listen to them, how do you think your rating would be? If you have found a relationship does exist between how well you get along with people and how well they listen to you (there usually is), then you may also have a better understanding of how other people feel about you when you don't listen to them.

Relationships require good communication if they are to last. Based on what you have learned, what role does listening play (its importance) in good communication and in developing healthy relationships?

* * * *

(A) Some Questions on Trust

As his trust in Dr. Balding grew, Jamie found, he was more easily able to share feelings with him. Answer the following questions regarding your experience with trust.

1. Have you ever told someone a secret and later found they didn't keep it? Describe what happened. It isn't necessary to identify the person.

2. How did you feel when you found out your secret was told to others.

3. Did you ever tell that person a secret again? Explain why you did/didn't.

4. What is your definition of trust?

5. Why is it important in sports that coaches and players trust each other?

6. Families in a way are like teams. What do they have in common?

7. Based on your experiences with friends and family, how do you get to the point where you can trust someone?

*   *   *   *

(A) Assuming Responsibility for Others

1. Do you believe Jamie was responsible for his parents' arguments and for his dad moving out? ____ yes ____ no

Explain the reason for your answer:

```



```

2. Select one of the two following statements, (a) or (b), with which you agree. Write why you believe this choice is more correct than the other.

(a) If we truly love someone, like a parent, we must also be willing to assume responsibility for that person's happiness and well being.

(b) It is important to be supportive to the people we care about. However, we must realize that their feelings belong to them. It is best not to assume responsibility for those things that are beyond our control.

```



```

3. It is often said that to be a responsible person is a positive quality. This is a true statement. What in your opinion is the difference between being a responsible person and being responsible for others?

4. Have you ever felt you were the cause of your parents' arguments? How did this make you feel?

*   *   *   *

(A) Poor Me

1. Dr. Balding explains to Jamie how some people choose to learn and grow from their painful experiences, while others choose to remain in their painful place, taking on a "poor me" attitude. Based on what you read in the text, describe in your own words a "poor me' attitude.

2. Why do you suppose some people choose to remain in a "poor me" place feeling sorry for themselves? What do they get out of remaining in that place (what's their payoff)?

3. Have you ever felt sorry for yourself, and then decided to do something about changing how you felt? What did you do to make the change?

4. The choices you make affect the direction you go in your life. Explain what positive choices you might make if you had been in Jamie's situation (experiencing emotional pain and feeling sorry for himself).

*   *   *   *

(A) How Good It Feels

As Jamie made changes and improvements, for the first time he liked the person he was. Can you remember making positive changes in yourself? For example: improving how you looked, your grades in school, how you did certain things or how you talked to people, etc. How good did you feel about it afterwards?

Describe the particular event or change that took place and how you felt about it.

Event or change:

How you felt afterwards:

(B) I Like Me and the World Is Beautiful

When positive personal changes are made, other good things usually happen. In Jamie's case, he began to like himself better and his whole life improved. How one views themselves (or likes themselves) is called self-concept. Have you ever noticed when you accomplished some goal or improved yourself, how your self-concept improved and the effect it had on your life?

Describe the event that improved your self-concept and the effect it had on your life.

The event:

The effect it had upon your life:

(C) Evaluating Self-Concepts

Explain what the term "self-concept" means to you. Describe the self-concepts of Jamie, Clarence, Marty and Diane during their earlier years. What is your self-concept today?

Self-concept means:

Describe Jamie's self-concept:

Describe Clarence's self-concept:

Describe Marty's self-concept:

Describe Diane's self-concept:

Describe your own self-concept as it is today:

*   *   *   *

CHAPTER NINE

NEEDING TO BE WHO YOU ARE
Coming Together As Equals

CONTENTS

CHAPTER SUMMARY

SIGNIFICANT POINTS AND OBJECTIVES

EXERCISE TOPICS
    Recognition and acceptance
    Brothers and sisters relating
    Negative comments and their effect
    Positive thoughts can quiet the inner critic
    Assuming responsibility for one's actions
    Personal values and strengths

CHAPTER SUMMARY

NEEDING TO BE WHO YOU ARE
Coming Together As Equals

Jamie and his family are excited about George coming home for the Thanksgiving holiday. The two brothers, George and Jamie, spend time together sharing experiences and their feelings regarding their parents' difficult times. George announces to Jamie that soon he will become engaged to a girl named Linda, who lives in California. Jamie, although happy for his brother, becomes sad at the prospect of losing him. As a part of their discussion, Jamie tells his brother of the hurt he has carried about his father making comparisons between the two of them. George empathizes with Jamie and assures him that he never realized that this was going on. Jamie shares the positive changes that have taken place for him as a part of his therapy, and George indicates how proud he is of him. Jamie indicates one of the most important lessons he has learned from his therapy is that he can't be another George, for he really needs to be himself.

• Before starting this chapter, review any questions the participants might have on issues covered in the previous session. This should be followed by group discussion of the current chapter.

SIGNIFICANT POINTS, OBJECTIVES AND EXERCISES

POINT #1

Jamie and his brother George go off alone to renew their relationship. Since George went away to college, Jamie misses the times they used to spend together.

OBJECTIVE

To explore:

- the importance of recognition and acceptance
- what it's like having or not having a brother or sister
- what it's like being an only child, the youngest child, or the oldest child

LEADER'S NOTES

The following exercises can be used to help the participants better understand their own sibling relationships and the effect these relationships have upon family dynamics. Many of the feelings and frustrations are universal, yet some relationships become closely bonded while others, full of anger and jealousy, become more distant. This exercise can provide value to the participants by having them better understand the importance of giving and receiving recognition and acceptance to loved ones and how brother/sister relationships function. Discussion can encourage exploring feelings directed toward understanding and improving sibling relationships.

In the first part of Exercise 1A, the group will focus on the positive feedback Jamie received from his older brother George regarding the changes that had taken place in Jamie since they last saw each other. The second part of Exercise 1A involves having the group explore a similar situation where they were commended for something they accomplished. An "or" situation has been included (question: What kind of comments would you like to have received?) to allow those young people who have either not received positive comments or can't recall any, to respond. Following this exercise, request input from anyone who wants to share information or feelings and then request group input on:

- Why was it important to Jamie that his brother acknowledge his positive changes?
- Why is recognition important?

As a part of Exercise 1B, compile on the chalkboard the group's results of their individual sibling survey in chart form (either line or bar graph) and seek input from the group on any other family position they think would be more desirable than theirs.

141

LEADER'S NOTES (continued)

For a more in-depth analysis of family dynamics, the group, as a part of Exercise 1C will individually construct their family trees. It would be helpful if you show a typical family tree on the chalkboard, as in the example provided.

In Exercise 1D, to help the participants with thoughts for their sub-group activity, they will list three reasons:
  (a) why they like or don't like having older or younger brothers or sisters
  (c) why they like or don't like being the youngest child, middle child, oldest child or only child

After they have written their reasons for liking or disliking their family position, the group is to be broken into sub-groups of all oldest children, all youngest children, all middle children and all only children. A recorder is to be selected by each sub-group, who will keep a record of the advantages and disadvantages of family position. When the sharing is complete, the recorders will report their findings to the overall group. Conclusions concerning similar themes and commonalties will be reviewed and summarized.

<u>Example of Family Tree:</u>
  <u>Mary</u> (mom) <u>Jane</u> (stepmother) <u>Edward</u> (dad) (include step-parents or an only parent and indicate who lives in their household)

Pete 17   Sandy 12   Sara 7   (include and identify
                                      any stepbrothers and
                                      stepsisters who live
                                      in their household)

EXERCISE #1
  (A) Making Discoveries
  (B) Compiling a Group Survey
  (C) Your Family Tree
  (D) Examining Family Positions

*   *   *   *

POINT #2

George expresses to Jamie how concerned he had been about Jamie putting himself down, and also how badly he felt about their father making negative comments about Jamie.

OBJECTIVE

To learn:

- how negative comments can affect conditioning
- how thinking positive thoughts can quiet the inner critic

LEADER'S NOTES

Negative and positive comments are often encountered in our dealings with others. Minimizing and coping with those negative comments is essential to our well-being. Focusing on positive thoughts can quiet the inner critic and enhance one's self-worth. The following exercise investigates positive/negative statements and how people react to them.

Exercise 2A explores how negative comments affected Jamie's and George's reaction to their father's treatment of Jamie. The question is asked "How do you feel those negative comments affected Jamie?" followed by the question, "What was George's reaction to his father's treatment of Jamie?"

In Exercise 2B, the group will be given a homework assignment for period of time (one to two days) to observe and record reactions to positive and negative comments that others might make to them. The assignment includes:

1. Recording any three positive and three negative comments made to you during the assigned period of time
2. How did you react when each comment was made to you?

They should also be aware and note their physical reactions, such as tensing up, moving away, facial expressions, etc. The group will share their reports, summarizing the similarities/differences between the responses and their reactions toward positive and negative comments.

Exercise 2C is a follow-up activity to Exercise 2B. The purpose is to illustrate that negative comments can be turned into positive comments just by being restated.

EXERCISE #2

(A) The Effects of Negative Statements
(B) An Investigation
(C) Making Positives Out of Negatives

*   *   *   *

POINT #3

Jamie explains to George that one of the things he learned in counseling is that no one can help him as much as he can help himself. Although he needs to be responsible for himself, Jamie gives credit to his counselor, "Without him, I'd still be blaming others for how I am."

OBJECTIVE

To explore:
  • the importance of assuming responsibility for one's actions

LEADER'S NOTES

The main focus of Exercise 3A through 3C is to examine the possible responsibilities young people may encounter and their perception of how well they deal with these responsibilities. Discussion can follow each of the exercises regarding what was written and what was learned.

In Exercise A, the group is asked to restate what Jamie told his brother he learned from counseling regarding personal responsibility. Chapter Nine, page 107 of the text states, "One thing I've learned is that no one can help me but me. I don't mean to take away from what I've learned from Jerry. Without him, I'd still be where I was, not liking myself and blaming others for how I am."

In Exercise 3B, the group is given the opportunity to rate how well they assume responsibility for the items listed by marking them from "excellent" to "needs improvement."

In completing these exercises on responsibility, Exercise 3C asks that they take some action by selecting two of those items rated as "needs improvement," listing them and writing a plan they could initiate in the next week or two that would help them improve in these areas of responsibility.

EXERCISE #3

  (A) Learning About Yourself Is Important
  (B) Responsibility Checklist
  (C) Making a Plan

*   *   *   *

POINT #4

Jamie said, "The most important thing I learned from my therapy, which I needed to understand, is that I could never be another George. As much as I love and admire you, I need to be me."

OBJECTIVE

To get in touch with:
- personal values and strengths

LEADER'S NOTES

With the many pressures and influences from others, young people have a difficult time being themselves. Added to these difficulties and pressures is the fact that they are just beginning to explore who they really are, in terms of being an adult or a child. They often try to emulate some real or fictional figure they admire. Focusing on personal strengths and values can bring about a greater appreciation for them. The basis for these exercises is to encourage focusing on one's strengths.

In Exercise 4A, the group will explore reasons why Jamie found it difficult to be himself (last paragraph page 107 and top of page 108 of the text). Upon completion of the written exercises, discussion will take place.

As an optional project, Exercise 4B has the group prepare individual collages based on their personal strengths. Have them add five descriptive words to the collage that emphasize their talents and strengths.

Exercise 4C contains a number of values on which group members will grade themselves using a scale of 1 to 10, with 10 being the highest score and 1 the lowest. When the ratings have been completed and totaled, have the group members turn in their total scores to you without personal identification. Have them help you total the group results and determine an average score. This score can then be written on the chalkboard with the accompanying comments shown below the exercise. The group members can then compare their results to the group average.

LEADER'S NOTES (continued)

In Exercise 4D, the group will list the two things they like most about themselves. Have them share this information with the whole group.

As a closure to Exercise 4, discussion should focus on the importance of getting in touch with personal values and strengths. Have them add any strengths they feel should have been on the list and were missing. Conclude the discussion with some input from them on how to improve their strengths.

EXERCISE #4

(A) Being Me
(B) The "Me" Collage
(C) Your Personal Values/Strengths Thermometer
(D) Things I Like Best

*   *   *   *

(A) Making Discoveries

George commented on how much Jamie had grown emotionally since he last saw him. What are some of the positive changes that had taken place for Jamie ?

```



























```

Recall a situation when someone important to you commented on something positive you accomplished. What took place and how did it feel to you; or what comments would you have liked to receive?

What took place?
How did it feel to you?
What comments would you have liked to receive?

(B) Compiling a Group Survey

In this exercise, you will participate in developing a group survey chart. It will show how many children there are in your family, whether you are the oldest, middle, youngest, or only child. Your information will be combined with the other members of your class to develop an entire group chart. The following information will be required:

How many children in your family? (include step and half brothers/sisters)

```
┌────────────────────────────────────┐
│                                    │
└────────────────────────────────────┘
```

Are you the youngest child in your family?

```
┌────────────────────────────────────┐
│                                    │
└────────────────────────────────────┘
```

Are you the oldest child in your family?

```
┌────────────────────────────────────┐
│                                    │
└────────────────────────────────────┘
```

Are you a middle child in your family? (older and younger sisters or brothers)

```
┌────────────────────────────────────┐
│                                    │
└────────────────────────────────────┘
```

Are you the only child in your family?

```
┌────────────────────────────────────┐
│                                    │
└────────────────────────────────────┘
```

(C) Your Family Tree

Prepare your personal family chart, showing all the members of your family. You will be given instructions on how to do this.

(D) Examining Family Positions

List three reasons why you like or don't like having older or younger brothers/sisters.

1.
2.
3.

List three reasons why you like or don't like being the youngest child, middle child, oldest child, or only child

1.
2.
3.

*   *   *   *

(A) The Effects of Negative Statements

George told Jamie how badly he felt when their father made negative comments about Jamie.

How do you feel those negative comments affected Jamie?

What was George's reaction to his father's treatment of Jamie?

(B) An Investigation

Record three positive comments and your reactions.

Comment	Reaction
1.	
2.	
3.	

Record three negative comments and your reactions

Comment	Reaction
1.	
2.	
3.	

List what you believe are the similarities and differences between the reactions to positive and negative remarks in the two activities above.

(C) Making Positives Out of Negatives

Choose any two negative statements from Exercise 2B. List them in the negative comment column below. Restate them in a positive way in the positive version column. See the following example to better understand how this is done.

Example: NEGATIVE: "Your papers are always messy." POSITIVE: "If you're more careful, I'm sure you will be able to write more neatly." OR, "In our class neatness is rewarded with 5 points for neat papers."

Negative comment	Positive version
1.	
2.	

*   *   *   *

(A) Learning About Yourself Is Important

Jamie shared with George some important things he realized about himself during counseling. What did Jamie learn regarding personal responsibility? See Chapter Nine, page 107 of the text.

(B) Responsibility Checklist

The following is a list of responsibilities that you may experience in your daily life. (No one else will look at this exercise, it is for your personal use only.) Rate yourself as honestly as you can on how well you meet these responsibilities. Rate each item from "excellent" to "needs improvement" by putting a check in the column that applies. If the responsibility listed does not apply to you, leave it blank.

Responsibility	Excellent	Very Good	Fair	Needs Improvement
1. do homework	☐	☐	☐	☐
2. do household chores	☐	☐	☐	☐
3. watch brother/sister	☐	☐	☐	☐
4. study for tests	☐	☐	☐	☐
5. clean room	☐	☐	☐	☐
6. perform after school job	☐	☐	☐	☐
7. take care of pets	☐	☐	☐	☐
8. help in family business	☐	☐	☐	☐

List two other responsibilities you have:

	Excellent	Very Good	Fair	Needs Improvement
9. _____	☐	☐	☐	☐
10. _____	☐	☐	☐	☐

(C) Making a Plan

Choose two items from those you rated "needs improvement." Write a plan you can initiate in the next week or two that would help you improve in these areas of personal responsibility.

Issue	Your plan
1.	
2.	

*   *   *   *

(A) Being Me

Jamie told George the most important thing he learned is that he could never be another George. Jamie told his brother "I need to be me." What are some of the reasons it was difficult for Jamie and others to "be me?"

```
_____
_____
_____
_____
_____
_____
_____
_____
_____
_____
```

(B) The "Me" Collage

Everyone has personal values and strengths. What are you good at? In what areas do you really shine? On a poster board, collect pictures or make drawings to illustrate these strengths. Arrange what you have collected in an interesting design on your poster board. Include five descriptive words that emphasize these talents/strengths.

(C) Your Personal Values/Strengths Thermometer

On a scale of 1 to 10, with 10 being the highest rating, rate yourself on the following items.

1. Personality (how well you get along with others) ☐
2. Appearance (how well you groom yourself) ☐
3. Intelligence (how bright you are) ☐
4. Talent (artistic, sing, dance, play an instrument) ☐
5. Fun to be with (people enjoy being with you) ☐
6. Self-motivation (interest in learning) ☐
7. Sense of humor (fun to be around) ☐
8. Loyalty (respects family, friends and authorities) ☐
9. Listening ability (willing to hear what others are saying) ☐
10. Speaking ability (able to convey thoughts and information) ☐
11. Punctuality (on time for appointments and school) ☐
12. Kindness (willing to help when needed) ☐
13. Caring (has empathy for family and friends) ☐
14. Honesty with self (willing to make changes as needed) ☐
15. Honesty with others (can be trusted) ☐
16. Student functions (pays attention in school) ☐
17. Responsibility (performs tasks at home) ☐
18. Judgment (knows right from wrong) ☐
19. Willpower (cannot be persuaded to do what is not right) ☐
20. Self-sufficiency (able to cook and take care of self) ☐

Total_____

Score: 200 perfect - best recheck your figures; after all, who's perfect?

    150-199 you've got a lot going for you

    130-149 on the road to reaching personal strength

    120-129 much better than average

    110-119 moving up

    100-109 room to improve

     90-99 halfway mark

     80-89 not bad

     60-79 could use improvement

    below 59, check low areas and prepare to improve personal strengths

(D) Things I Like Best

Think about yourself as a person and complete the following statement.

The two things I like most about myself are:

1.
2.

*   *   *   *

CHAPTER TEN

WHEN PARENTS LIVE APART
Two Thanksgiving Dinners

CONTENTS

CHAPTER SUMMARY

SIGNIFICANT POINTS AND OBJECTIVES

EXERCISE TOPICS
    Family holidays
    Parenting issues
    (Optional Topic)
    Parent dating issues

CHAPTER SUMMARY

WHEN PARENTS LIVE APART
Two Thanksgiving Dinners

Jamie and George wonder how two thanksgiving dinners, one at their mother's and another at their father's, will be for them. Their concerns about their mother being alone for the holiday are lessened when they find out that their aunt and uncle have been invited to dinner. That evening, after enjoying their first dinner with their mother, Jamie and George leave for their father's place for what is to be their second meal. At first, Jamie is surprised and then has a strong negative reaction to meeting his father's friend Marian. On the way home from their father's, George tries without much success to explain their dad's position, but Jamie is unable to accept that his father has a girlfriend. Jamie becomes angry at Marian, who he believes wants to take his father away from his mother and break up their family. He also feels quite upset with his father, whose actions indicate he is happy with Marian.

• Before starting this chapter, review any questions the participants might have on issues covered in the previous session. This should be followed by group discussion of the current chapter.

SIGNIFICANT POINTS, OBJECTIVES AND EXERCISES

POINT #1

During the first year of their mother's and father's separation and with their parents living in different households, Jamie and his brother question how they will handle two Thanksgiving dinners.

Holidays can be full of pressure and stress for many people. It is a time when loneliness, family concerns and expectations can cause upset and even depression.

OBJECTIVE

To explore:
- family holidays and what emotions they evoke in the individual
- personal attitudes on parenting (identifying qualities they would like to have when they become parents)

LEADER'S NOTES

It is recommended that you begin this activity with a relaxation exercise to help focus your group's thoughts on the various holidays that are meaningful to them. Encourage them to visualize themselves experiencing each holiday as they write, thus making it easier for them to identify their feelings related to each chosen holiday.

It may be helpful if you set the tone by first sharing your experience of a particular holiday that is significant to you and how you felt on that day. The same basic leader information applies to Exercise 1A and 1B.

Exercise 1A asks the participants to list their three most meaningful holidays (those they and their family celebrate) in the order of importance to them and why they like that holiday.

Exercise 1B asks for a list of the holidays that are less important or not as enjoyable and their reasons. Discussion of holidays, reason for choice, and feelings should follow.

LEADER'S NOTES (continued)

Exercise 1C involves the question of parental preparation for two holiday dinners, first from the standpoint of Jamie's parents and then from their own perspective (if they were parents, what they would do). This exercise can be followed by group discussion or by role playing the parent/child handling of this situation.

EXERCISE #1
(A) Important Holidays and Feelings
(B) Least Important Holidays and Feelings
(C) Jamie's Two Thanksgivings

*   *   *   *

POINT #2

When Jamie first meets his father's lady friend, Marian, he is upset and unfriendly to her. Jamie sees Marian as a threat to his family and he believes being friendly to her would be unfair to his mother.

OBJECTIVE

To explore:
- why Jamie felt so upset regarding his father and Marian
- individual feelings concerning parent dating

LEADER'S NOTES

Exercise 2A contains six writing assignments using the text to have the group better understand Jamie and his father's feelings regarding Marian coming into his father's life. In the last portion of this exercise the group has the opportunity to indicate whether Jamie's father might have handled the situation differently. It is recommended that discussion and/or any feelings relating to this situation follow these exercises.

Exercise 2B can be assigned as homework. It provides the group with a movie project for which they are to write a script. The story involves two characters, a parent and a child, and their discussion (using first person dialog) of the child's feelings regarding the separated parent starting to date. Notebook paper should be used for this project, following the example shown in the exercise.

LEADER'S NOTES (continued)

In Exercise 2C, the group is told to rewrite the ending so that there is a happy conclusion to this movie, if the story did not result in a happy ending for both parties. This portion of the exercise can also be assigned for homework.

Exercise 2D asks the group to write their feelings from two perspectives; first, from the perspective of the child, and then, from the parent's position. The wrap-up of these exercises could include role-playing some of the scripts and finally, some feedback from the group on what they have learned from being able to put themselves into both the parent and child role.

EXERCISE #2
(A) Please, No Surprises
(B) A Screenplay on Parent Dating
(C) Rewriting the Screenplay with a Happy Ending
(D) Screenwriters and Others Must Understand Feelings

*   *   *   *

(A) Important Holidays and Feelings

Jamie and his brother experienced strong feelings about their parents being separated and the need to split their Thanksgiving dinner by spending time with each of them.

Many young and old people are affected by holidays in different ways. The following exercise may help you better understand how certain holidays affect you. List three holidays which you and your family celebrate. List the most important holiday first, then write the feelings you have for that particular day or your reason for liking that holiday.

Holidays (most important first)	Feelings or reasons
1.	
2.	
3.	

(B) Least Important Holidays and Feelings

Which holidays do you like the least or are are the least important to you? List these three holidays, with #1 being the one you have the most trouble enjoying. Next to each holiday listed, write your reasons and feelings for not liking that holiday.

Holidays (least liked first)	Feelings or reasons
1.	
2.	
3.	

(C) Jamie's Two Thanksgivings

Describe how Jamie felt about having to celebrate Thanksgiving twice the year his parents separated, once with his mother and then with his father. Can you relate to the feelings Jamie had experienced? Do you think his parents prepared him for his first holiday apart? If so, in what way?

Imagine that you are a parent in a similar situation. How would you prepare your child for the first holiday your family was not going to celebrate together?

*   *   *   *

(A) Please, No Surprises

Jamie was shocked when he met his father's friend Marian. Reread pages 113-114 in the text. Answer these questions in your own words:

1. What took place when Jamie first met Marian?

2. Why was Jamie so unfriendly to Marian?

3. How do you think you might have felt in a similar situation?

4. If you ever experienced a similar situation, how did you react?

5. Summarize in your own words the conversation Jamie, George and their father had in the bedroom. Begin the summary with Jamie's father asking his sons to go into the bedroom with him so he could explain some important things to them.

Jamie's father told them:

6. Do you feel Jamie's father handled the situation well? Why?

(B) A Screenplay on Parent Dating

In this exercise you can call upon your own personal experiences or create an imaginary situation. Make believe you have been asked to write a script for a new movie. The scene involves two characters, one, a parent (either mother or father), and his/her children. The parents in the story are not living together. In this scene, the parent is asking the child what his/her feelings would be if the parent started dating.

Write the characters' names on the left side of the page. The dialog is written on the right side following the example below. Use notebook paper for writing your script.

__mother__

> Since your father and I have been divorced, I've been thinking about dating other men. How would you feel if I started dating?

(C) Rewriting the Screenplay with a Happy Ending

If your outcome had the parent or the child feeling badly, write a new ending that leaves both parties feeling good. In other words, in this script have the two characters in the movie finish their discussion feeling better than they did when they began.

(D) Screenwriters and Others Must Understand Feelings

Write about your feelings, imagining you were the young person in the story. Use only the script with the happy ending.

Write about how you felt, imagining you were the parent in this situation.

* * * *

CHAPTER ELEVEN

LEARNING TO FACE LIFE
Breaking Out of the Fear Cycle

CONTENTS

CHAPTER SUMMARY

SIGNIFICANT POINTS AND OBJECTIVES

EXERCISE TOPICS

CHAPTER SUMMARY

LEARNING TO FACE LIFE
Breaking Out of the Fear Cycle

Jamie returns to Dr. Balding for assistance in dealing with the entry of Marian into his father's life. Through the counseling that takes place, he learns why he has reacted to Marian so strongly. Jamie also gains an understanding of his fear of people. A major breakthrough takes place for Jamie in his work with Dr. Balding as he realizes how fear has controlled him and affected his life. He learns about the "Fear Cycle," how it functions, and the importance of breaking out of it. Jamie makes a giant step forward in his personal growth by choosing to deal with his fear (in this case, the loss of his dad). After getting together with his father and Marian, Jamie realizes that Marian is a nice person. George once again returns to school and to his girlfriend Linda. Jamie's parents' divorce becomes final and, although he remains supportive to his mother, he now realizes that he cannot be responsible for what takes place, for his parents' situation is beyond his control. As a result of his growth, he is able to feel much better and see himself in a new and more positive light.

• Before starting this chapter, review any questions the participants might have on issues covered in the previous session. This should be followed by group discussion of the current chapter.

SIGNIFICANT POINTS, OBJECTIVES AND EXERCISES

POINT #1

Jamie explains his upset feelings about his mother and father possibly not getting back together because of Marian. Dr. Balding points out to Jamie that no one can predict or be responsible for the outcome of a situation beyond their control.

OBJECTIVE

To recognize:

- the difference between situations that are beyond one's control and those that are not

LEADER'S NOTES

Exercise 1 contains a group of activities geared toward helping the group understand the difference between situations beyond their control and those in which they can control the outcome. Learning to be and feel responsible for ourselves and our own actions, as opposed to the actions of others (situations beyond our control), is a learning task that doesn't come easily for anyone including adults. The process of recognizing one from the other comes easier when the learning begins early.

In Exercise 1A, the group looks up in the text (page 116) the statement in which Dr. Balding tells Jamie, "Jamie, it's your fears that are blocking you concerning your parents." Then, the participants are asked to copy the statement which follows and answer the questions: What was Jamie's biggest fear? Do you think Jamie could control the outcome of this problem? What are your reasons?

Answer: 1. "And you're going to need to get past them, before you can comfortably get on with the rest of your life."

2. Jamie's biggest fear was that his parents would never get back together.

LEADER'S NOTES (continued)

Exercise 1B asks the group to explore those situations in their own lives (or their families') that are beyond their control. It begins with a personal journal home assignment (their journal activity should not be required to be shared). Then, have them list five situations of any kind that would be beyond their control, e.g., parents arguing, needing to pay taxes, death, floods, earthquakes, when someone else is sad or angry, who their brother or sister will be, their favorite football team losing, etc.

Exercise 1C is the opposite of 1B. In this exercise, the group lists five situations that can be controlled by the individual, e.g., can control their own anger, how they feel about themselves, how well they do in school or at work, what career they choose to follow, who they marry, or, if they get married, etc.

An anger controlling activity takes place in Exercise 1D, followed by a reflection of how they felt having dealt with some angry feelings they were carrying.

Exercise 1E is used for group sharing on any part of Exercise 1 that has been completed and also for sharing what they have learned regarding the difference between actions and behaviors they can and cannot control. This would be a good place for you to point out the similarities between what they have learned regarding (1) what can be controlled, and, (2) being responsible for the actions, behavior and feelings of oneself instead of for others.

EXERCISE #1

(A) Jamie's Biggest Fear
(B) Situations I Cannot Control
(C) Situations I Can Control
(D) An Anger-Controlling Exercise
(E) Controllable or Uncontrollable?

*　　*　　*　　*

POINT #2

Dr. Balding describes the "fear cycle" and how people often choose not to deal with the situations they fear, hoping that they will go away.

It's important to understand that those fears that aren't dealt with don't go away. Instead, the opposite often occurs and the fears grow stronger and larger. Note: the fear cycle is described on page 117 of the text.

OBJECTIVE

To understand:
- how the "fear cycle" functions and how to break out of it
- how to best deal with fear

LEADER'S NOTES

Prior to beginning this exercise, a discussion of fears with your group would be helpful, including recapping what they learned in Chapter Three pertaining to fear. Chapter Three, Exercise 1A covered new situations and fear; Exercise 1B, reasonable and unreasonable fears; and Exercise 1C, how fear can control one's ability to function.

In Exercise 2A, the group can use the text as reference, but should rewrite Dr. Balding's explanation of the FEAR CYCLE in their own words. (Have them reread pages 117-120.) After they rewrite the meaning, (action must be taken to free oneself of a fear, otherwise it remains with the person and the fear grows stronger) group discussion should follow to strengthen their understanding of how it functions.

For Exercise 2B, have the group write five fears that affect their school life, home life, or social life. Then have them call out these fears while you list them on the chalkboard. Do not erase this list as it will be used again in Exercise 3.

EXERCISE #2

(A) The Fear Cycle
(B) A Fearsome Brainstorming Activity

*   *   *   *

POINT #3

Jamie recognizes how his fear of losing his father and his family is affecting his relationship with his father and Marian. He chooses to face his fear head-on by developing a plan of action and calling his father to arrange to get together with him and Marian.

OBJECTIVE

To understand:

- the importance, when making personal changes, of developing an action plan and following through on that plan

LEADER'S NOTES

For Exercise 3A, have the group use their list of fears from Exercise 2B and add to each identified fear a first step course of action for diffusing it (diffusing is the term Dr. Balding uses in his conversation with Jamie, top of text page 120).

When they have completed their list of fears and actions to be taken, group discussion should follow regarding the various forms of action (write them on the chalkboard next to the fears that were previously listed, use general action terms instead of more personal forms of action that may be called out). Seek additional input that may add value to the action items stated.

Close this exercise with further input from the group, seeking clarification and assurance of understanding that the only way to deal with fears that are affecting our ability to function or to make positive choices is to face those fears, one at a time, and diffuse their power by taking some form of action.

EXERCISE #3

(A) Taking Action

*   *   *   *

POINT #4

Jamie tells Dr. Balding that he hasn't felt this good about himself for as far back as he can remember. "Can you believe it, I actually feel proud of myself," he says.

Feeling good about oneself, pride of accomplishment, and self-motivation are all related.

OBJECTIVE

To explore:

- how self-satisfaction results from making positive changes in oneself
- problem solving strategies
- the importance of self-acceptance

LEADER'S NOTES

Exercise 4A deals first with why Jamie was feeling proud of himself (page 124 of the text), and then has the group writing about the last time they felt proud of themselves by describing the experience and the steps that led to the feeling. Closure should include discussion directed at how making positive changes brings about feelings of self-satisfaction, pride, and well-being.

Exercise 4B includes a process for problem-solving. Individually, the group writes a current problem they are fearful of. Closing their eyes, they allow their minds to focus on the problem and all of the options they can think of for resolving that problem. After listing the available options, they then list the consequence or results of applying each option. After evaluating all of their options and their results, they select their choice, one of their options, which they feel is best for resolving their problem. With this done, they now write their reason for choosing the option they did.

In Exercise 4C (Pride in Accomplishment), they write how it feels to come up with a possible resolution to their problem.

Exercise 4D reminds the group how good Jamie felt about himself after making positive changes in his life and then asks that they describe what self-acceptance means to them and why it is important. Conclude this exercise and the chapter with sharing of information and feelings.

EXERCISE #4

(A) Pride and Self-Satisfaction
(B) Problem-Solving
(C) Pride in Accomplishment
(D) What Is Self-Acceptance?

*   *   *   *

(A) Jamie's Biggest Fear

1. Dr. Balding told Jamie that to overcome his fears he had to first be willing to honestly face those fears.

Turn to page 116 in the text. Locate the paragraph that begins with the sentence, "Jamie, it's your fears that are blocking you concerning your parents." Now, write the next sentence on the lines below:

2. What was Jamie's biggest fear?

3. Do you think Jamie could control the outcome of this problem? What are your reasons?

(B) Situations I Cannot Control

1. Have you ever found yourself being fearful of something beyond your control? If so, writing about it can be quite helpful. You can use the following PERSONAL JOURNAL LOG (at home) to write about the incident. This journal is for your eyes only; it's up to you to decide if you want anyone else to read your personal writing.

PERSONAL JOURNAL

2. List five situations you feel you're not able to control.

   <u>Examples:</u> (1) Jamie couldn't control how his parents felt about one another. (2) Jamie couldn't control Clarence taking an overdose of pills.

1.
2.
3.
4.
5.

(C) Situations I Can Control

List five situations you feel capable of controlling.

<u>Examples:</u> I am capable of controlling the way I express my anger by (1) screaming silently or by exercising really hard. (2) crunching up a letter I wrote, getting all my angry feelings out, and then throwing it into the trash.

1.

2.

3.

4.

5.

(D) An Anger-Controlling Exercise

Using notebook paper, write a letter to someone you feel angry at or something you feel angry about. Express all of your feelings. Tell him/her why you're angry and what you're angry about. When you feel finished and have said everything you wanted to say about the issue, then crunch up the paper as hard as you can and throw it into the trash.

It is important to throw it away as soon as you complete it, to be finished with it. REMEMBER: WRITE IT, CRUNCH IT, and THROW IT AWAY. This is a constructive way for dealing with anger, because it gets you in touch with your feelings. You release your anger and also any frustration that sometimes accompanies it. Otherwise, you might feel powerless to do anything about your anger.

Immediately following this exercise, close your eyes and relax. Get in touch with how you feel after having expressed your anger. Now, briefly write about how you feel. (Are you feeling better after having dealt with your anger?)

(E) Controllable or Uncontrollable?

As a group, we will discuss what has been learned regarding the difference between what we are able to control (need to be responsible for) and what is beyond our control (what we don't need to be responsible for). Before the start of the group discussion, you may make some notes of those points that you want to mention.

Points for discussion:

*   *   *   *

(A) The Fear Cycle

Use pages 117-120 in the text as a reference. In your own words, describe the "fear cycle" and how it functions.

(B) A Fearsome Brainstorming Activity

List five things you fear that affect your life in school, at home or with your friends.

FEARS

1.
2.
3.
4.
5.

*   *   *   *

(A) Taking Action

The first step in resolving any problem is to develop a plan of action. This plan includes:

> (a) brainstorming and listing the problem
>
> (b) listing the options available for taking action

By taking these two steps, you have begun the process of taking action.

Your action plan calls for you to list your five fears from Exercise 2B. Then add some form of action that you might take to overcome the fear.

Example:

> Fear: losing dad to Marian   Action: having dinner with dad and Marian to get to know each other better

	FEAR		ACTION
1.	-		
2.	-		
3.	-		
4.	-		
5.	-		

*   *   *   *

(A) Pride and Self-Satisfaction

In the last paragraph on page 124 of the text, Jamie speaks proudly of himself. In the following space, write why you think he was feeling so good about himself.

When was the last time you felt proud of yourself? Describe the experience and the steps that led to that feeling.

(B) Problem-Solving

Think of a problem you have in your life right now in which you feel fearful. If you can't think of one, create an imaginary one for this exercise. State the problem: _____

_____

Now, clear your mind by closing your eyes. Allow your mind to focus on the problem and how you can resolve it. List all of the alternatives (options) you can think of that can help you resolve the problem in a positive way. Write them in the space provided. Next to each option, write the possible results of this action.

OPTION	RESULTS

Think about your choices (options) and the consequences (results). Choose the one option that would bring about the most overall positive results and of which you would feel proud . Write your selection below and why you chose it.

My choice for resolving the problem is:

My reason for choosing this option is:

(C) Pride in Accomplishment

The steps you have taken to resolve the problem you selected above are something you can remember and apply for solving other problems that may occur in your life. Sometimes problems or fears seem too big for us to deal with. However, like Dr. Balding said, if we face them one at a time, they don't seem to overpower us. Writing about the problem and its possible solutions is developing an action plan. This allows one to focus on the problem, the options for resolving it, and taking the first step to overcome it.

Think about the problem you worked on above and the possible solution you have come up with. By using your imagination and looking into the future a little, see yourself putting the plan you came up with into action. Get in touch with how it feels to know that you have resolved a problem that has been bothering you. In psychological terms, what you have accomplished is called "growth," or making positive changes in your life.

How do you feel about following a plan that was successful?

If you feel dissatisfied, you can choose another alternative and follow it through. The important point is to allow yourself the freedom to explore your options. There are no mistakes. All of your choices teach you how to evaluate your problem from another viewpoint and to resolve your problems more successfully the next time.

(D) What Is Self-Acceptance?

Jamie began feeling good about himself and began to like who he was when he made positive changes. Through your own experiences, describe what self-acceptance means to you and why it's important:

| |
| |
| |
| |
| |
| |
| |
| |
| |
| |
| |
| |
| |
| |

*   *   *   *

CHAPTER TWELVE

CHANGES IN RELATIONSHIPS
A Time for Saying Goodbye

CONTENTS

CHAPTER SUMMARY

SIGNIFICANT POINTS AND OBJECTIVES

EXERCISE TOPICS
    Self-motivation
    Self-confidence and its effect on personal relating
    Providing and receiving guidance

CHAPTER SUMMARY

CHANGES IN RELATIONSHIPS
A Time for Saying Goodbye

A few winters pass, and with them, a number of changes take place for Jamie and his family. George, after completing college, goes on to graduate school. He and Linda are married and they decide to settle in California. Jamie's father and Marian are also married, and his mother and a man named Fred are making plans for their future. Jamie graduates from Farnsworth Jr. High and enters Washington High. The new Jamie is motivated and able to place greater focus on his studies. Becoming more confident in himself, he also finds it easier to be with and enjoy people. Jamie and Diane, whose relationship has grown closer, are now showing signs of change. At the insistence of Diane's parents, who feel that Diane and Jamie should have the opportunity to meet and date other young people, Jamie and Diane unwillingly agree to conclude their exclusive relationship. Making the best of their situation, they both become active and popular in high school. Diane uses cheerleading as her outlet, and Jamie, still gaining confidence, becomes a quarterback on the football team.

• Before starting this chapter, review any questions the participants might have on issues covered in the previous session. This should be followed by group discussion of the current chapter.

SIGNIFICANT POINTS, OBJECTIVES AND EXERCISES

POINT #1

As the new Jamie appears, he becomes motivated and is able to concentrate more on his studies.

OBJECTIVE

To understand:
- how Jamie and others like him become self-motivated
- the value of being self-motivated

LEADER'S NOTES

The following exercises pertain to feeling better about oneself through self-motivation. Before starting the exercises, direct your group to reread Chapter 12 of the text. Then have them answer the questions in this exercise, using complete sentences. Inform them that they can refer to the book as they answer the questions. Discussion should follow each question. Especially significant would be a discussion of the importance of self-motivation and how your group might apply it to their lives.

Exercise 1A asks the participants: What and who helped Jamie most to overcome his negative feelings? They are then asked to select two improvements from the list provided that were the most important to Jamie in overcoming his poor self-image and to explain why.

ANSWER:

Answers may vary. However, it is important for the group to understand the significance of: Jamie's willingness to seek help, the value of his counseling experience, and the supportiveness of Ms. Richards.

Exercise 1B asks: What does the term "self-motivated" mean to you? Why is it important? What is its connection to how a person feels about himself/herself? (Self-concept)..

Exercise IC asks the participants to think about a time when they were self-motivated and to describe what took place. Did you feel you were better at what you did because of your motivation? How did you feel about your accomplishment?

LEADER'S NOTES (continued)

Exercise 1D asks them to think about some other areas of their lives in which their self-motivation is not too strong. Describe what needs improvement.

Why has your self-motivation not been working well? What could you do to improve your level of motivation?

Exercise 1E asks: What do you think are the most important values to be gained from self-motivation?

ANSWER:
Group should be guided toward understanding that self-motivation will directly affect all aspects of one's life: academic, social and personal.

Exercise 1F concludes this exercise by having the participants develop an action plan for improving their lives by implementing what they have learned in this exercise regarding self-motivation.

A SPECIAL NOTE ON SELF-MOTIVATION

The key to success depends on personal motivation. Motivation provides you with reasons for doing things, getting things done, and then feeling good about your accomplishments and yourself. Motivation is a very personal thing. Making money, feeling good about yourself, having pride, being creative, helping others, being popular, being physically fit, having fame, and having power are all sources of inspiration tied to motivation. What motivates you may be one of these, a combination of several of these, or something totally different. The important points for you to remember are:

(1) motivation will move you to the position and future you desire for yourself

(2) without motivation, you will have a difficult time reaching your goals

(3) the strongest motivation of all is when we motivate ourselves

EXERCISE #1
(A) Feeling Better About Oneself
(B) The Results Can Be Great
(C) With Self-Motivation
(D) Improving Self-Motivation
(E) Important Values to Be Gained
(F) Personal Action Plan

* * * *

196

POINT #2

As Jamie becomes more confident in himself, he finds it easier to be with and relate to people.

OBJECTIVE

To understand:
- how self-confidence affects one's ability to relate to others

LEADER'S NOTES

This exercise involves individual exploration of self-confidence and relating, first through written assignment, and then through discussion in triads. When the triad portion is complete (approximately 10 minutes) ask the whole to share what they have learned or if they may have gained some different view of anyone they know who is lacking confidence. The questions include:

1. Describe in your own words what self-confidence is.

2. Why do you think Jamie's improved self-confidence had such a positive effect upon his ability to relate to others?

3. Describe how a person might act with other people when they have little confidence in themselves.

4. List some of your thoughts as to what might cause low self-confidence.

5. What do you think could be done to improve self-confidence?

6. For your PERSONAL JOURNAL (which doesn't need to be shared with others but can be shared if you choose to), describe your own level of confidence. What are you doing or will you do to improve it as a part of your action plan?

EXERCISE #2

(A) Self-Confidence and Relating

*   *   *   *

197

POINT #3

At Diane's parents insistence that she date others, she and Jamie stopped going steady.

Young people may have strong feelings about what they feel is parents intruding in their lives. Adults may see their role and the action they take as required parental guidance. These opposite views are the source of many family conflicts. There are different opinions regarding whether one has the right to intrude and enforce or provide firm guidance, and to what age.

OBJECTIVE

To explore:
- attitudes and feelings regarding the position Diane's parents took on Diane and Jamie's relationship
- effective (acceptable) methods for providing and receiving guidance

LEADER'S NOTES

Exercise 3A is comprised of three writing assignments and a role-playing exercise.

1. The group will reflect on how it felt from Diane and Jamie's perspective when Diane's parents insisted that Diane date other boys. Then they provide three reasons why the parents' view was not good.

2. Following discussion on what they came up with, the group will change roles and offer their feelings and reasons from the parents' perspective.

3. The participants once again assume the role of the parent and write their view as to what is the proper stance parents should take in regard to involving themselves in their children's decision-making and to what age.

Exercise 3A concludes with role-playing of both positions, followed by discussion directed at what caring parents can do to be most effective in the guidance they provide, and at the same time, to offer workable solutions to all concerned. Some important points to be made during the discussion are: the value of putting oneself into the other person's position (understanding); the difficulty (as a loving parent) of providing sound guidance, although knowing it may be unpopular and cause conflict; and being nonjudgmental of the other party.

EXERCISE #3

(A) The Parent Role

*　*　*　*

(A) Feeling Better About Oneself

1. It became a lot easier for Jamie to motivate himself and to concentrate on his learning with out his negative feelings. What and who helped Jamie most to overcome his negative feelings?

2. Choose from the list below the two improvements you think were most important to Jamie in overcoming his poor self-image. Why? Select your first and second choices in order of importance by marking "1" and "2" in the boxes below.

He learned to:
☐ be a good listener
☐ solve problems
☐ accept the feelings of others
☐ overcome his fears
☐ feel better about himself
☐ more easily express his feelings
☐ take positive action
☐ _____ other (describe)

Give your reason(s) for choice #1

```
_____
_____
_____
_____
_____
_____
_____
_____
_____
_____
```

Give your reason(s) for choice #2

```
_____
_____
_____
_____
_____
_____
_____
_____
_____
```

(B) The Results Can Be Great

Jamie's self-concept and self-confidence improved. His work habits and grades also improved as a result of his becoming self-motivated. What does the term self-motivated mean to you? Why is it so important? What is its connection to how a person feels about himself/herself?

Self-motivated means:

It is important because:

It usually goes along with self-concept because:

(C) With Self-Motivation

Think about some time when you were self-motivated. It could have involved something at school, at home, at work, with friends, in sports, or even in your social life. Describe what took place. Do you feel you were better at what you did because of your motivation? How did you feel about your accomplishment?

A time when I was self-motivated:

How my motivation affected me:

How I felt about my accomplishment:

(D) Improving Self-Motivation

Now, think about some other areas of your life in which your self-motivation is not too strong and as a result of it, the quality of what you have done has been affected. Describe what it is that needs improvement. Why has your self-motivation not been working too well in this case? What could you do to improve your level of motivation?

What needs improvement?

Why hasn't your self-motivation been working too well in this area?

What might you do to improve your self-motivation?

(E) Important Values To Be Gained

What do you think are the most important values to be gained from self-motivation?

(F) Personal Action Plan

Now that you have learned about self-motivation, how would you apply or put into action what you've learned to improve yourself for today and the future

Action plan:

*   *   *   *

(A) Self-Confidence and Relating

When Jamie began feeling better about himself, his ability to talk to and listen to others improved. He found that relating to girls, especially Diane, also improved.

1. Important changes took place for Jamie connected to his gaining self-confidence. Describe in your own words what self-confidence is:

```
_____
_____
_____
_____
_____
_____
_____
```

2. Why do you think Jamie's improved self-confidence had such a positive effect upon his ability to relate to others?

```
_____
_____
_____
_____
_____
_____
```

3. Describe how a person might act with other people when they have little confidence in themselves:

```
_____
_____
_____
_____
_____
_____
```

4. List your thoughts as to what might cause low self-confidence:

```
_____
_____
_____
_____
_____
_____
```

5. What do you think could be done to improve self-confidence?

```
_____
_____
_____
_____
_____
_____
```

PERSONAL JOURNAL

6. For your PERSONAL JOURNAL (which doesn't need to be shared with others, but can if you choose to), describe your own level of confidence. What are you doing or will you do to improve it as a part of your action plan?

* * * *

(A) The Parent Role

1. Jamie and Diane were unhappy when Diane's parents told her that instead of dating only Jamie, she was to see other boys as well.

Put yourself into Jamie and Diane's place. Pretend that your parents are telling you that you shouldn't go steady at such an early age and that you should date others. Describe how it feels to you, and then list three reasons why Diane's parents' view is not correct.

How it feels:

Three reasons:

1.

2.

3.

2. Now, as much as possible, let go of the feelings you have in understanding Jamie and Diane's position and put yourself into the role of thinking as Diane's parents. Describe your feelings as a caring parent, seeing your child going steady with one person and never having dated anyone else. List three reasons why Diane's parents position, that she date other young people, is a good one.

How it feels:

Three reasons:

1.

2.

3.

3. You have been in both positions, first as Diane and Jamie, understanding how they might have felt, and then as Diane's parent, experiencing the feelings from another view.

It may have been somewhat difficult for you to put yourself into the parent role, because you haven't been one yet. As a future parent, it could be valuable for you to better understand how hard it is at times for responsible and loving parents to provide guidance they know will create conflict between them and their children.

There is a fine line for parents between being responsible and involved in the process of their children's growth and development and overstepping that responsibility by restricting young people's ability to learn to make decisions and choices on their own.

Thinking of yourself as a parent once again, state your feelings regarding how involved you would be in your children's lives (telling them what is best for them) and to what age would you continue.

* * * *

CHAPTER THIRTEEN

PEER PRESSURE AND DRUGS
Marty's Crazy Stunt

CONTENTS

CHAPTER SUMMARY

SIGNIFICANT POINTS AND OBJECTIVES

EXERCISE TOPICS
    Peer acceptance
    Using drugs and alcohol
    Peer group rejection
    Value of learning from one's experiences

CHAPTER SUMMARY

PEER PRESSURE AND DRUGS
Marty's Crazy Stunt

Marty, still needing to prove himself and to be accepted by the older kids, is convinced by them to do a crazy stunt. His latest and wildest scheme involves smoking pot in the principal's office. As a result of his foolish adventure, he gets expelled from school and restricted by his parents. The hardest punishment for Marty to accept is being laughed at by everyone at school. When his period of punishment ends, Marty is offered the option of transferring to another school, yet he chooses to return to Washington High. Jamie respects Marty and the courage he shows in being willing to come back to the school where he has been the laughingstock. That particular experience becomes Marty's turning point. He uses that period as one to learn from, making many changes, including to not smoke dope again. Changes continue to take place with Jamie's family. His mother and Fred are married,and his father, with whom Jamie finally succeeds in building a close relationship, relocates to California after a period of illness.

• Before starting this chapter, review any questions the participants might have on issues covered in the previous session. This should be followed by group discussion of the current chapter.

SIGNIFICANT POINTS, OBJECTIVES AND EXERCISES

POINT #1

Marty does almost anything to prove himself and to be accepted by the older kids.

Many young people, in their need to be accepted by their peers, experiment with drugs. Marty is an excellent example of how childish prodding and peer pressure work with some people.

OBJECTIVE

To explore:
- Marty's need for acceptance from his peers
- why some teens use drugs and alcohol, while others don't

LEADER'S NOTES

Adolescents become involved in drugs because: they want to be accepted by their peers, poor self-esteem, parental pressures, rebellion, and in an attempt to escape from reality. Many causes of drug involvement are related to one another. Although wanting to be accepted by their peers and the pressure applied by that group (peer pressure) are usually singled out as the strongest causes, when a young person feels good about themselves it becomes easier to resist pressures.

Exercise 1A asks for three reasons why Marty chose to get involved in drugs and three reasons for Jamie chosing not to. The participants then tell why someone they know is taking drugs. They then pick any two reasons (for Marty or the person they know) for taking drugs and provide alternatives or suggestions to help that person say no. Group sharing and discussion should follow.

Exercise 1B states: Marty was easily teased into taking risks and using drugs, because he wanted acceptance from his peers. This exercise asks the group to select three reasons, out of ten possible answers provided, why Marty or people like him have such a need for acceptance. They are then asked why they selected the answers they did. Group sharing and discussion should follow.

Answer: #2, #7, and #9 are best answers

EXERCISE #1

(A) Marty's and Jamie's Views on Drugs
(B) Marty's Need for Acceptance

* * * *

POINT #2

Marty is expelled from school and restricted by his parents from all outside activities. The most difficult part of this experience for Marty is being rejected by his so-called friends.

OBJECTIVE

To explore:
- feelings concerning peer group rejection

LEADER'S NOTES

Peer pressure is largely associated with the fear of rejection. Most young people want to be "in" with their age group, whether the focus is on clothes, hair styles, movies, or music. This type of group pressure, which is mostly self-induced and occurs from wanting to belong and to be accepted, distracts the young person from his/her search for individual identity. The influence of the group becomes the stronger need. Along with wanting to belong, are concerns of not being accepted, or being rejected by one's peers.. Through a voting process, this exercise explores how group judgment (being different) can influence one's personal attitudes.

In Exercise 2A, each participant votes for their favorite musical group from the list provided, or they can add a name. They write their choice on a piece of paper, anonymously and submit them to you. Recap the results for use in Exercise 2B.

Exercise 2B is a consensus activity. Divide the group into sub-groups of five and direct them to come up with one favorite musical group, in ten minutes. A spokesperson for each group reports their group's selection. Write the results on the chalkboard for comparison with the voting that took place in Exercise 2A.

Exercise 2C is a Personal Journal activity. It is not meant to be shared, except voluntarily. Besides explaining how consensus works (example: trial jury), it explores feelings regarding peer pressure influence, which result in loss of freedom of choice. How the Soviet political system functions is an analogy. People there don't need to worry about where to work or live because those choices are

made for them However, in living under that form of government, they give up many of their freedoms, including making decisions for themselves.

Exercise 2D is a group recap activity focusing on what has been learned regarding:
- group influence
- group rejection
- freedom to make choices
- individuality
- active or passive in group interaction

216

EXERCISE #2

(A) Your Favorite Musical Group

(B) Group Favorite

(C) How Does It Feel?

(D) Sharing What You Learned

* * * *

POINT #3

Jamie respects Marty for his courage in deciding to return to his old school where he was laughed at before being suspended. For Marty, his terrible experience brings him much learning and growth.

OBJECTIVE

To understand:

how value is gained when one learns from experiences

LEADER'S NOTES

Exercise 3A asks the questions: 1) What did Marty learn from his crazy stunt? and 2) Why did Jamie see Marty differently after he returned to the same school?

Exercise 3B asks the group members to recall and write about a particular experience in their lives that resulted in learning more about themselves (what was the experience and what did you learn from it?). Following their writing, have each person select a partner and share their experiences and what they learned from it. Then ask for voluntary sharing with the whole group.

Exercise 3C has the group think about someone they have known who tends to repeat his/her mistakes. If that person was willing to listen, what advice would they give? The response relates to Exercise 3C, which says: Mistakes not learned from tend to be repeated. Ask for sharing of the situations and suggested advice.

EXERCISE #3

(A) Learning the Hard Way

(B) Recall an Experience

(C) Mistakes Not Learned from Are Often Repeated

* * * *

(A) Marty's and Jamie's Views on Drugs

1. During high school, Marty was easily influenced to take drugs, while Jamie was not. Why do you think Marty got into drugs and Jamie didn't? List your three reasons:

Why Marty did:
1.
2.
3.

Why Jamie didn't:
1.
2.
3.

2. If there is anyone you know who's involved in drugs or alcohol, why do you think he/she is?

3. Choose any of the two reasons from above, regarding why people are taking drugs. List some possible alternatives or suggestions you would give this person to help them say no to drugs.

Reason	Alternatives
1.	
2.	

(B) Marty's Need for Acceptance

Marty was influenced and teased by some of the kids at school into doing some wild things, including taking drugs. Some teasing remarks are:

"Come on. It won't hurt you to try it."

"All the kids are doing it."

"The coolest kids smoke and that's what you need to do to be a part of the crowd."

Marty allowed other kids to dare him to do things and tease him, because he wanted to be accepted. Why do Marty and others like him need so much to be accepted? A number of possible reasons are listed below. Pick three you think are the most accurate.

Marty wanted to be accepted because:

#1 ☐ he liked people

#2 ☐ he didn't have much confidence in himself

#3 ☐ he was a people-pleaser by nature

#4 ☐ being liked meant doing what people wanted

#5 ☐ he liked being a part of the "in group"

#6 ☐ he was shy

#7 ☐ he wanted to prove that he was their equal

#8 ☐ he wanted to be popular

#9 ☐ he had a poor self-image

#10 ☐ he was a bully

Now tell why you chose those three.

1st choice   # _____

2nd choice # _____

3rd choice   # _____

*   *   *   *

(A) Your Favorite Musical Group

In this exercise, you will have the opportunity to vote for your favorite musical group. This will be a secret ballot, so don't compare your answer with others and don't write your name on the ballot. Select one musical group from those listed below. If your favorite is not listed, write it in.

☐ U2   ☐ Prince
☐ Michael Jackson   ☐ Run D.M.C.
☐ The Beastie Boys   ☐ A-Ha
☐ The Bangles   ☐ Bon Jovi
☐ Genesis   ☐ Duran Duran
☐ Judas Priest   ☐ New Order
☐ Huey Lewis & The News   ☐ Depeche Mode
☐ David Bowie   ☐ Bruce Springsteen
☐ Iron Maiden   ☐ Lionel Richie
☐ Madonna   ☐ O.M.D.
☐ _____   ☐ _____
☐ _____   ☐ _____

Why do you like this group best?

Write your selection of your favorite musical group on a piece of paper and hand it in to your group leader.

(B) Group Favorite

You will receive instructions on this activity.

(C) How Does It Feel?

PERSONAL JOURNAL

This is your Personal Journal activity. Your response to the following questions need not be shared with anyone, except if you choose to do so. For you to get the most value, your answers to the questions in this activity will require you to get in touch with how you feel.

1. Did you feel comfortable during the consensus exercise asking that your favorite group be the one selected? _____ YES _____ NO

Explain why:

2. Was your vote influenced by the other members of your group? _____ YES _____ NO   Explain how you felt during this process.

3. How does it feel when you are alone in your actions and not a part of the group?

_____

4. Compare how you felt voting alone with how you felt when you were voting in a group. What was the difference for you?

_____

5. Is it more difficult for you to make decisions in a group as opposed to when you are alone? _____ YES _____ NO   Explain:

```
_____
_____
_____
_____
_____
_____
_____
_____
```

6. Young people, like Marty, are sometimes influenced by their friends to do things that are harmful to them. What could you do to resist peer pressure and not lose your ability to make your own decisions? What might influence you to do things that are not really your own choice of right or wrong (your values)?

```
I would resist peer pressure by:
_____
_____
_____
_____
_____
Things that might influence me to go against my values:
_____
_____
_____
_____
_____
```

7. Examine your actions in the group's process of reaching an agreement regarding which musical group to select. Did you try to influence your group with your selection (taking an active role) in the consensus activity, or did you take a less active role, waiting for others to make the decision (more passive role)?

_____ACTIVE   _____PASSIVE

If your role was "active," explain how it felt and what motivated you. If your role was more "passive," explain how that felt and if fear of rejection influenced how you reacted within the group.

(D) Sharing What You Learned

As a part of this activity, everyone will share what has been learned regarding group influence and rejection, freedom to make choices, individuality and being active or passive in group interaction.

*   *   *   *

(A) Learning the Hard Way

Marty learned a lot from his terrible experience (his crazy stunt) by returning to school after his suspension. He knew he would once again be made fun of by the other kids. However, he still decided to go back and face them in order to make changes in his own life.

1. What do you think Marty learned from his crazy stunt?

2. Why did Jamie see Marty differently after he decided to return to the same school?

(B) Recall an Experience

Think back to some experience in your life that resulted in your learning more about yourself.

What was the experience?
What did you learn from it?

(C) Mistakes Not Learned from Are Often Repeated

The wise men of India have been credited with saying that all experiences in life, both good and bad, are meant to be learned from. One's mistakes can only carry value if they result in learning, for those that are not learned from, tend to be repeated.

Have you ever known anyone who tends to repeat his mistakes? Based on what you now know, if that person was willing to hear what you had to say, what advice might you give him/her?

* * * *

CHAPTER FOURTEEN

GROWING OLDER AND HOPEFULLY WISER
And the Seasons Passed

CONTENTS

CHAPTER SUMMARY

SIGNIFICANT POINTS AND OBJECTIVES

EXERCISE TOPICS

CHAPTER SUMMARY

GROWING OLDER AND HOPEFULLY WISER
And the Seasons Passed

In overcoming many of his insecurities, Jamie begins to like the person that he is and to enjoy the pleasures of his life. Time moves more quickly for him, and the story takes us forward in time to Jamie as an adult. Five years after graduating from college, Jamie is married, and with the continued passing of time, he becomes the father of two boys and a girl. Following the birth of his first son, Jamie prays that when his child grows up, he will not experience the pain he did. To help those prayers come true, he also makes a promise to often remind his child of his love for him. Jamie recognizes the importance, through his own experiences, of having his children feel loved and understood. His hope is that they will never need to ask, "Why can't anyone hear me?" Alone with his thoughts, Jamie once again reflects upon his youth and as he does he stares at his big oak tree, which now stands tall and strong in his backyard. He realizes that this tree has always been important to him, very much like an old friend who, while quiet and strong, continues to change and grow. During this period, Jamie and his family visit California, where he is reunited with the Western branch of his family and once again is able to enjoy feelings of closeness with his father and brother.

• Before starting this chapter, review any questions the participants might have on issues covered in the previous session. This should be followed by group discussion of the current chapter.

SIGNIFICANT POINTS, OBJECTIVES AND EXERCISES

POINT #1

In college, Jamie notices that many kids he meets are either going through their crazy phase like Marty had, or are loners and frightened as he had been.

OBJECTIVE

To explore:
- how self-esteem affects one's behavior
- the importance of learning from one's experiences

LEADER'S NOTES

Exercise 1A involves developing an understanding of what self-esteem is. First, the participants write their definitions for self-esteem and then, through open discussion and inputs (using the chalkboard) a group definition is established. The participants, after listing the group definition in their workbook, compare the group's understanding of the term with their own and describe the major difference between the two. They are also asked to list three factors that affect how one feels about oneself, good or bad. Discussion should follow each activity to ensure that everyone understands self-esteem.

Note: There may be many correct and different answers to the definition, still the essence of self-esteem which affects people's behavior, has to do with how people feel about themselves. How one feels about himself or herself changes with their experiences (successes and failures). As people strengthen themselves and their self-esteem, they are not as strongly affected by their failures, using them instead as tools by which to learn.

For Exercise 1B, the statements found in Chapter Fourteen of the text are to be completed, using the multiple choices provided. Following the individual writing activity, answers should be agreed upon through group discussion. The participants are then asked to provide a written response to: Why self-esteem is something with which everyone should concern themselves. Having established what self-esteem is, its importance and its relationship to behavior, the last portion of this exercise involves the more personal question of what steps might be taken to improve how they feel about themselves. All parts of this exercise should conclude with discussion. Voluntary sharing time should be allotted for question three, dealing with personal self-improvement.

Answers: Multiple choice answers in sequential order are: e, d, e and a.

EXERCISE #1
(A) Understanding Self-Esteem
(B) Self-Esteem and Behavior

*   *   *   *

POINT #2
Jamie, through the years, feels a special connection with the big oak tree in his backyard. To him, the tree is like a good friend, one with whom he has grown up and who has always been there with him. Jamie admires its quiet strength and state of constant change.

OBJECTIVE
To explore:
- the meaning and application of metaphors
- the growth of Jamie's tree as a metaphor for human growth
- nature's seasons as a metaphor for the changes and development within one's life (used in the text as major section breaks and as major periods within Jamie's life)

LEADER'S NOTES
Exercise 2A covers the meaning of metaphors and their application to life situations.

1. Start by providing a definition of the term "metaphor" for your group. Webster's Dictionary defines a metaphor as "a figure of speech in which a term is transferred from the object it ordinarily designates to an object it may only designate by implicit comparison or analogy, as in the phrase "evening of life." After giving a few examples, ask the group to offer some examples of their own. Example: The moon shined brightly upon his house (good things happened to him).

2. The participants are asked what Jamie was talking about when he said: {I admire its quiet strength and its state of constant change" (the tree in his backyard).

3. The four seasons (used in the text as metaphors for the major periods of change in Jamie's life), are provided as a form of metaphor to create ideas on how nature's changes can relate to human changes. An example is provided for Springtime.

4. The preceding activity is expanded upon by asking what lessons are to be learned from the metaphor of the tree that not only survived the bitterness of

LEADER'S NOTES (continued)

the seasons, but also grew tall and strong as well. Discussion following this might assist those who have difficulty understanding the analogy as meaning: Through the years of human growth there are happy times and sad times, easy times and hard times (life has its ups and downs). Yet, as a result of all of these times and experiences, there is the opportunity for us all to grow wiser and stronger.

Exercise 2B provides some closing thoughts, as well as the significant learning from this exercise, by discussing metaphors and life.

EXERCISE #2
(A) What's a Metaphor?
(B) Some Important Thoughts on Metaphors and Life

*   *   *   *

POINT #3

George explained to Jamie his decision making process for revising his career goals. "First, I did as much analysis as I could, weighing all of the pros and cons, then when it got right down to it and I still felt somewhat confused, I did what usually works best for me, I trusted my feelings."

OBJECTIVE
To explore:
• methods for helping the decision making process

LEADER'S NOTES
Exercise 3A deals with learning to make decisions and provides sentence completion questions tied to the text and personal exploration of decision-making. This exercise works well as a combination of individual input to the questions and sharing of information in diads. The small group activity allows each point to be discussed and each individual's process for decision making shared.
  Answer: question 1, he trusted his feelings

EXERCISE #3
(A) Learning to Make Decisions

*   *   *   *

233

(A) Understanding Self-Esteem

Jamie's self-esteem improved and his whole life improved as well.

1. Write your definition for "self-esteem."

2. Write the definition for "self-esteem" decided on by the group.

3. Is the class definition different from your personal definition? If so, what is the major difference?

4. The way Jamie and his friends felt about themselves did not remain the same. Sometimes people feel good about themselves and other times they feel badly. List three factors that can affect how a person feels about himself or herself (good or bad)

1.

2.

3.

(B) Self-Esteem and Behavior

1. Multiple choice: Circle the correct answer as it directly relates to the reading of Chapter Fourteen of the text.

When Jamie went to college, he observed that other students.
   a. were frightened, just as he had been several years before.
   b. were reading in the library.
   c. were going through a crazy phase like Marty had gone through.
   d. were eating lunch on the lawn.
   e. both a and c.

It was a lot easier for Jamie to understand how the other students felt during those college years because
   a. he talked to other students about his feelings.
   b. he read books on the subject.
   c. he was extremely sensitive.
   d. he had lived through what most of them were experiencing.
   e. his therapist helped him see how others felt.

Jamie learned a lot during those difficult years. He became more
   a. secretive with friends.
   b. outgoing.
   c. selective in choosing friends.
   d. inquisitive when talking to friends.
   e. emotional during difficult times.

It was a rough four years for Jamie because
   a. he missed his family very much.
   b. he had to work evenings while going to school.
   c. other students gave him a hard time.
   d. his teachers didn't understand his feelings.
   e. he had to work hard at maintaining the grades he wanted.

Graduation was a real high for Jamie because
   a. he had a real sense of personal accomplishment.
   b. he was able to go to California and visit his brother.
   c. he knew he wouldn't need to stay up late studying anymore.
   d. his entire family and his girlfriend would be at the ceremony.
   e. he had taken drugs.

2 Consider what you have learned about self-esteem and its effect upon people's behavior and how they interact with others. Why do you feel self-esteem is something with which everyone should concern themselves?

```
_____
_____
_____
_____
_____
_____
_____
_____
_____
```

3. Through changes in Jamie's life, he improved his self-esteem, which had positive results for him. What steps do you believe you could take to improve how you feel about yourself?

```
_____
_____
_____
_____
_____
_____
_____
_____
_____
_____
_____
```

* * * *

(A) What's a Metaphor?

1. Discussion on what a metaphor is and how it's used. (Group leader will explain)

2. Jamie said "I admire its quiet strength and its state of constant change." What was he talking about? _____

3. He also said that springtime is a time when living things take root and begin to change and grow. Label each of the seasons with a feature of nature, how it changes, and then a human change (some change in your life or that of others) that you can relate to which ties in to the seasonal change. Follow the example for springtime shown below. The springtime example for the human change says: Falling in love. Falling in love is used because of the expression: "In the Springtime, a young man's fancy turns to thoughts of love."

SEASON	FEATURE	CHANGE	HUMAN CHANGE
Springtime	Trees	Blossoms turn green	Falling in love
Winter	_____	_____	_____
Summer	_____	_____	_____
Fall	_____	_____	_____

4. As the years moved on and the seasons changed, Jamie saw his tree also grow and change. In spite of the hard times (dry summers and extremely bad winters), the tree still grew strong and tall. There is a metaphor here in comparing ourselves to this tree. Explain what lessons might be learned by comparing oneself to a tree that not only survived the bitter times of the seasons, but also grew strong and tall.

(B) Some Important Thoughts on Metaphors and Life

Hopefully, you've learned how metaphors and the events of life compare. The following questions may be easy for you to answer. However, the information which they contain, although very important to understand, is sometimes not as easy to accept. Answer yes or no.

Does life constantly change? _____

Can we learn from our experiences? _____

Can those experiences prepare us for future experiences? _____

Is human growth similar to nature in any way? _____

If you answered "yes" to all those questions, you are right. However, the importance is in understanding, so please review the following:

Each event in your life can affect how you deal with other events. Our lives prepare us with steppingstones for our future. Just as Jamie's tree, standing strong and tall withstood the weather and swayed with the wind, so can we learn to flow with life's changes.

*   *   *   *

(A) Learning to Make Decisions

Making decisions (like choices) is important in every aspect of one's life. Most situations require decisions to be made. Some decisions may not be too important because their results will not have a strong or lasting effect upon you.

Example: Should I have a grilled cheese sandwich or a hamburger for lunch?

Other decisions can be very important to you.

Example: Should I focus on math in school and direct myself towards becoming an engineer or should I concentrate on science and chemistry to become a doctor.

1. Jamie's brother, George, in talking about his decision-making process said, "First I made as much analysis as I could, weighing all the pros and cons, then when I got right down to it and still felt somewhat confused, I did what usually works best for me, I:

> | |
> | --- |

2. Think about the last decision you made. Describe it:

> | |
> | --- |
> | |
> | |
> | |

3. How do you feel about that decision? Explain:

> | |
> | --- |
> | |
> | |
> | |

4. How did you make that decision? Did you trust your instincts or go against them?

5. Think of some other decisions you have made in your life. What did you do in each of these situations that was similar?

6. Prepare a list of the three most important decisions you have made this year. Looking back at them, were they good decisions or not? Did you listen to and trust your feelings/instinct when you made them?

a.

b.

c.

7. What is the most important point you've learned about making decisions?

* * * *

CHAPTER FIFTEEN

LEARNING FROM HAPPINESS AND PAIN
Some Things Don't Seem to Change

CONTENTS

CHAPTER SUMMARY

SIGNIFICANT POINTS AND OBJECTIVES

EXERCISE TOPICS
    The effect of positive choices
    The meaning of happiness and success
    The value of planning and goal-setting
    How to use goal-setting process

CHAPTER SUMMARY

LEARNING FROM HAPPINESS AND PAIN
Some Things Don't Seem to Change

Upon his return from California, Jamie recognizes that although he will miss George, his father, and their families, he is also happy to return home where life with his family and friends is so meaningful to him. Jamie, as an adult, allows his thoughts to return to his friends and the changes that have taken place in their lives. Marty, having survived the many problems of his youth, has learned well from those problems. After graduating with honors from high school, and then the university, Marty becomes a successful attorney. Clarence too is successful, only in a different way. Following graduation from high school, he does exactly what he has always dreamed of doing, he opens his own business. Clarence marries and continues to live in the same town where Jamie and he grew up, and they remain the best of friends. Jamie, using Clarence as an example, thinks about the true meaning of success. The two remaining characters who Jamie brings us up to date on are Diane and himself. Jamie now teaches school at Farnsworth, his old junior high, where he remains associated with Ms. Richards, who is still teaching there. Jamie and Diane, his childhood sweetheart, after resolving their difficulties, marry and share the joy of their children, their lives together, and the memories of their youth. The story closes with Jamie running down his old street on his way to work, fantasizing an image of Marty as a young boy tossing his ball in the air and shouting as he had so many times in the past, "Hey, Jamie baby, wanna play?" Jamie, with a grin on his face, replies, "I sure do, Marty, I sure do."

• Before starting this chapter, review any questions the participants might have on issues covered in the previous session. This should be followed by group discussion of the current chapter.

SIGNIFICANT POINTS, OBJECTIVES AND EXERCISES

POINT #1

Jamie, as an adult, reminisces about his friends from his youth and the changes that have taken place in their lives. He thinks of Marty, who completely changes his life, following his crazy stunt in high school. Marty, after graduating with honors from high school and then college, becomes a successful attorney.

Marty is a positive example of how people can change and overcome their conditioning when they make up their minds to do so.

OBJECTIVE

To focus on:
- the effect of making positive choices upon one's future and how this relates to self-esteem

LEADER'S NOTES

Exercise 1A consists of eight questions, focusing on the value of making positive choices, their effect upon one's actions and behaviors, and how it all ties in to how one feels about himself/herself (self-esteem). The written portion of this exercise can be assigned as homework, with follow-up discussion on the activities taking place in group.

The first six questions pertain to the events and characters in the story. The last two questions relate to how this information applies to self-esteem. as follows:

Question seven: What have you learned from this chapter and the story regarding the following true statements?
- Events, actions, behaviors and feelings affect self-esteem.
- Self-esteem can affect the choices and decisions we make.
- Choices and decisions affect how we live our lives.

The participants are asked to include information from these three facts in their written statement on what they have learned from this chapter.

Question eight: How might the information in this exercise be applied to help you improve the choices you make, your self-esteem, and your life in general?

EXERCISE #1

(A) Making Positive Choices

* * * *

245

POINT #2

Looking at the changes Clarence has made in his life is exciting to Jamie, because he sees Clarence as having become successful. Marty has also become successful, only in a different way. Jamie connects Clarence's success with being happy in what he is doing. In Clarence's case, having his own business meant doing exactly what he wanted to do.

OBJECTIVE

To explore:

• the meaning of happiness and success

LEADER'S NOTES

Exercise 2A deals with the issues of success and happiness, starting with Jamie's understanding of what success is (Chapter Fifteen, pages 152 and 154).

1. The participants are asked to define what success means to them.

2. Jamie felt happiness was an important part of success. The participant's are asked for their own meaning of the term "happiness."

3. Calls for the participants to list two people they know, or have heard of, who they feel are successful. Three columns are provided for analyzing the success of these people.

First column — <u>Name</u>, first name or initials are okay

Second column — <u>Elements,</u> identify three elements of success for each of the two names (might include: accumulated wealth, happy, healthy, respected, well-known in profession, head of large organization, attained goals, etc.).

Third column — <u>Category</u>, Place the following symbols next to each of the elements:

> P — power
> W — wealth
> H — happiness
> A — accomplishments
> O — other

Fourth column — <u>Score</u>, rate each of the success elements to be rated from 1 to 10, with 10 being the highest score. The grand totals will include the addition of all coded scores.

4. The participants analyze their results by selecting and explaining the highest coded score (assuming it was most important because they rated it highest). The same is then done for their lowest score.

LEADER'S NOTES (continued)

5. The participants are asked: Would you like to be successful someday, and in what way?

6. Eight personal characteristics or actions for professional success are provided. The participants are asked to select the most important one for achieving success. They are also to explain the reasons for their selection.

The discussion and group interaction following this exercise is important for sharing of views on this significant subject. The exercise will work equally well by breaking up into small groups, followed by a summing up in the whole group, or doing the whole process in the large group.

EXERCISE #2
(A) The Meaning of Success and Happiness

*　　*　　*　　*

POINT #3
Jamie accomplishes his goals by becoming a teacher at his old junior high and marrying his childhood sweetheart Diane.

OBJECTIVE
To focus on:
   • the importance of setting goals
   • how to apply goal setting

LEADER'S NOTES
Exercise 3A, dealing with learning about goals, consists of eight questions and is one of the more important participatory involvements in this *Guide*. In this chapter, the groundwork is laid for an understanding of what goal-setting is, why it is important, and how it is applied. In Chapter Sixteen which follows and is the concluding chapter, the participants will utilize what they have learned by preparing goals for themselves.

LEADER'S NOTES (continued)

Each of the following seven questions and the discussion which follows, attempts to bring about some understanding of goals.

1. What is a goal?

2a. Why do we need goals?

2b. Describe what might take place when someone attempts to accomplish a major task without a goal.
    Answer: 2a - Sense of direction
            2b - Wouldn't know how to get to where they want to go, how much effort is required, and when they will arrive (no plan)

3a and 3b. Ask questions that pertain to when Jamie first needed to start setting goals in order to meet his dream of being a teacher and how his use of goals helped him.

3c. After dealing with the importance of Jamie using goals, the participants are asked: When and how do you use goals?

4. What are some of the different types of goals?
    Answer: 4 - The correct answers for the (a) column in sequential order
            are: 7, 4, 5, 9, 8, 1, 3, 2 and 6.

5. What are the barriers to goals? Using a trip as an example, the participants are asked to come up with five potential barriers to reaching their destination and five solutions for overcoming these obstacles. The barriers might apply to problems with: the car, the highway, weather conditions, or the driver, etc.

6. Why is it important to understand what your barriers are?
    Answer: 6 - It is important so people can more easily overcome them and get back on track. As in the example of the loud bang in the car, they would be better off knowing and concentrating on the real problem (the tire) than putting their energy and time into something else that could distract them from reaching their goal. The more one is aware of and understands the problems they face, the better their chances of overcoming them.

7. How does one get started using goal-setting? Using an alarm clock for waking up to go to school as an example of goal setting that they most probably now are using, the participants are asked to list three other goals they have used prior to today.

Exercise 3B focuses on long and short-term goals. The essence of this exercise is to stress the importance of reducing longer-term goals to shorter increments (goals) that are more easily achievable and measurable.

1. Come up with six short-term goals that would have been appropriate for Jamie in working towards his long-term professional goal of becoming a teacher. There are many answers they may choose, including improved study habits to improve grades (an extra half hour of study each night).

2. Explore their own personal and professional objectives and come up with five long-term goals. There are a wide range of acceptable objectives from which they can select. Some examples are: to improve my bowling score by a 20-pin average, to improve my next report card to contain no fails, to develop more friends in school (next semester to have one more friend), to buy a car (get a job next summer and start saving), etc. Select one of long-term goal and write five short-term goals for it. These should be specific steps or actions they could take toward achieving their long-term goal.

EXERCISE #3
(A) Learning About Goals
(B) Long and Short-Term Goals

* * * *

(A) Making Positive Choices

As Jamie's, Diane's, Clarence's and Marty's stories unfold, you the reader are told how these young people lived and experienced the results of the choices and decisions they made. One of the important lessons presented in their stories is that the direction one takes in life can be changed by feeling better about oneself and by making positive choices. The following questions and group discussion focuses on making positive choices and how those choices affect a person's life.

1. Jamie's visit to California was great, but he was also happy to be home. Who picked him up at the airport?_____

What did Jamie think about as he drove home from the airport?

2. Jamie went on to say that his past had inspired him.

What did he mean by that statement?

3. Jamie reflected on the past, thinking about his friend Marty and the positive changes Marty made for himself.

(a) How would you describe Marty as a young boy?

(b) How would you describe Marty as an adult?

(c) What caused Marty to reevaluate his life and change it for the better?

4. The changes Marty made for himself affected his relationships with his friends and family.

How were those relationships affected?

5. What career did Marty choose as an adult?_____

If Marty had chosen not to change, how might his life have been different?

6. The experiences people go through in their lives often affect how they feel about themselves (their self-esteem). How one feels about himself/herself then affects their behavior and the choices they make.

(a) How did Marty feel about himself as a teenager?

(b) Why did Marty have so much trouble making and keeping friends?

7. What have you learned from this chapter and the story regarding the following true statements?

      (a) Events, actions, behaviors and feelings affect self-esteem.

      (b) Self-esteem can affect the choices and decisions we make.

      (c) Choices and decisions affect how we live our lives.

Include information on these three facts in your written answer.

8. How might the information in this exercise help you improve the choices you make, your self-esteem, and your life in general?

*   *   *   *

(A) The Meaning of Success and Happiness

1. In Chapter Fifteen, page 154 of the text, Jamie offers his definition of the term *success*. He also explains that success means different things to different people. What does success mean to you?

2. Jamie felt that happiness was an important part of success. Assuming this is so, it would be important to determine what happiness is. Describe what happiness means to you:

3. (a) List two people you know or have heard of, who you feel are successful. Use first names or initials only.

   (b) List the three most important elements of their success.

   (c) Choose the categories below that best describes their element of success.

   (d) Rate each category from 1 to 10, with 10 being the highest or strongest rating.

Categories are:

       P= power (political or people connections)

       W= wealth (money and/or property)

       H= happiness (enjoys his/her life: occupation, family and friends)

       A= accomplishments (author, artist, inventor, or human services)

       O= other (anything which doesn't fit under other categories)

(a) Name	(b) Elements of Success	(c) Category	(d) Score
_____	1. _____	____	_____
	2. _____	____	_____
	3. _____	____	_____
_____	1. _____	____	_____
	2. _____	____	_____
	3. _____	____	_____

Totals   P = ____

W = ____

H = ____

A = ____

O = ____

Grand Total _____

4. Which category has the highest total score? _____
   Do you believe that category has the most important parts of success?
   Explain:

Which has the lowest total score? _____
Do you believe that category has the least important parts of success?
Explain:

5. Would you like to be successful someday? In what way?

6. Select one of the personal characteristics or actions listed below that you feel is most important if a person is to achieve <u>professional success</u>. Explain why you feel it is the most important of those listed.

creativity   working to goals
working hard   honesty
enjoying work   intelligence
happiness   persistence

I believe that _____ is the most important item of those listed for achieving professional success.

The reason for my choice is:

*   *   *   *

(A) Learning About Goals

In the prior exercise, we explored the term *success*. I believe you would agree that to accomplish something meaningful for oneself (personal or professional success), one would need to develop goals.

Jamie accomplished two of his long-term goals that affected his future: to become a teacher at his old junior high, and to marry his childhood sweetheart Diane. Goal-setting is a necessary process for us all if we have a desire to progress in our lives.

As you learn how to use this powerful tool (goal-setting), you must understand some important points. By answering and understanding the following questions, you can start using the goal-setting process to achieve greater success in your life.

1. What is a goal?
2. Why do we need goals?
3. When and how do you use goals?
4. What are some of the different types of goals?
5. What are the barriers to goals?
6. Why is it important to understand what your barriers are?
7. How does one get started using goal-setting?

1. What is a goal? According to Webster's Dictionary, a goal is "the purpose towards which an endeavor is directed; an end; objective; the finish line of a race." To help you better understand what a goal is, list three goals that you and/or your family have recently used and how it worked for you or them.

Goal	How it worked
(a) _____	_____
(b) _____	_____
(c) _____	_____

2. (a) Why do we need goals?

2. (b) Describe what might take place when someone attempts to accomplish a major task without a goal.

3. (a) When do you think Jamie first needed to start setting goals to accomplish his dream of being a teacher?

3. (b) How did Jamie's use of goals help him?

3. (c) Now that you understand how Jamie used goals, when and how do you use them?

4. There are all kinds of goals that people deal with on a day-to-day basis. Match up the various types of goals or information applying to them (a) with the purpose or meaning of these goals (b). Put the numbers from column (b) in the boxes in column (a).

(a) <u>Types of Goal</u>

☐ short-term goal
☐ long-term goal
☐ realistic goal
☐ unrealistic goal
☐ milestone
☐ school goal
☐ career goal
☐ personal goal
☐ negative goal

(b) <u>Purpose of Goal</u>

1. to complete assignment
2. to be married and have a family
3. to become an engineer, teacher etc.
4. a future plan
5. a goal that can be accomplished
6. to break the law
7. to take a near-term view
8. to have important completion dates
9. to have frustration

5. What are the barriers to your goals? An easy way to explore this is to think of any goal as being similar to a destination or objective on an auto trip. The place that you have chosen to go might be difficult to find without having a road map to follow. In the example used above, what kind of barriers might occur on the way that could delay you in reaching your destination? (Could apply to your car, yourself, or something on the highway).

Think about a trip you might take and describe five possible barriers (obstacles) along the way. Describe a solution for overcoming each of them on the way to your destination (goal):

Barrier	Solution
1.	
2.	
3.	
4.	
5.	

6. Why is it important to understand what your barriers are? Use the driving example once more; if you think of the obstacles as being barriers to reaching your destination (goal), then it may become easier for you to understand their importance. You're driving on the highway, using your map to guide you, all off a sudden there is a loud bang. The thoughts that enter your mind are that it could be a tire problem (a blowout) or a problem with the motor. Why do you feel it would be important that you know (understand) what the problem is?

7. How does one start using goals? You may realize after learning about goal-setting that you have used goals before without knowing it. Now we will learn how to start using goals more effectively, by learning as much as you can about how to apply goal-setting and then start using it.

List three goals you have used for yourself prior to today. (Example: using an alarm clock to wake up at 6:30 a.m., Monday through Friday, to go to school)

1. _____

2. _____

3. _____

(B) Long and Short-Term Goals

1. The more you make plans in advance and establish goals, the better you can control the outcome of the significant events in your life. It is important when setting long-term goals (like a 3,000 mile trip across the country) to also have a number of short-term goals that you can focus on to keep you motivated. Without the short-term goals to keep you going in the right direction and to monitor how well you're doing, you could easily get sidetracked and lose interest.

   Jamie had two long-term goals: one personal, to marry Diane; the other professional, to teach at his old junior high. For the following activity, list Jamie's long-term professional goal and then provide six short-term goals you think would have been important for him to have had to keep him on track.

   LONG-TERM GOAL: _____

SHORT-TERM GOALS

1.	
2.	
3.	
4.	
5.	
6.	

2. In developing goals for yourself, keep in mind that goals should be:

<u>achievable</u> - doesn't make sense to have a goal you feel is impossible

<u>a challenge</u> - if it's too easy, you might get bored

<u>measurable</u> - goals must always have a form of measurement, otherwise they are open-ended and lose their meaning as goals. It is important that they include such forms of measurement as: what will be done, how will it be done, who will do it, when will each task be done, and what is the deadline

<u>specific</u> - it is difficult to focus on goals that are too general; being more specific allows for greater focus

Prepare a list of five long-term goals. These goals should involve things (either personal or professional) you would like to accomplish.

LONG-TERM GOALS

1.	
2.	
3.	
4.	

Now, select one of these goals and write five short-term goals for it. These should be actual steps or actions you would take toward reaching your long-term goal.

SHORT-TERM GOALS

1.	
2.	
3.	
4.	
5.	

*   *   *   *

CHAPTER SIXTEEN

(Covers Chapters Sixteen and Seventeen of the Text)

EXPLORING HAPPINESS AND GROWTH
and
IMPROVING YOUR RELATIONSHIPS
THROUGH POSITIVE ACTION

CONTENTS

CHAPTER SUMMARY

SIGNIFICANT POINTS AND OBJECTIVES

EXERCISE TOPICS
    Making choices
    Attitudes and positive beliefs
    Using Affirmations
    Dealing with stress and tension
    A personal plan for achievement

CLOSURE

CHAPTER SUMMARY

(Covers Chapters Sixteen and Seventeen of the Text)

EXPLORING HAPPINESS AND GROWTH
and
IMPROVING RELATIONSHIPS THROUGH POSITIVE ACTION

With Jamie's story now completed, we move on to the non-fiction part of *Why Can't Anyone Hear Me?* and a review of the many important issues covered in the text. One of the major points covered in Chapter Sixteen is exploring happiness and growth. The comparison is made once again between the growth of the tree and human growth. The importance of nurturing the growth of the tree and the individual is discussed. If the nurturing has included sufficient love and care, they mature independently strong. Also stressed is the need for programs such as the one in which this group has been involved (Teen Issues). Topics covered include: the need for more social education and preparation involving conflict resolution, developing relationships, parenting, coping with stress, learning how to relate to others, and how to improve oneself. Success is also discussed once more, with the point made, "With a better understanding of the self, interaction with others will come easier, and the elusive butterfly of happiness that everyone keeps chasing may come to rest on your shoulder."

The major points covered in Chapter Seventeen are: making choices for yourself, examining the "poor me" attitude, creating your reality through positive beliefs, relieving stress and tension, evaluating rules and limits and developing a support system.

• Before starting this chapter, review any questions the participants might have on issues covered in the previous session. This should be followed by group discussion of the current chapter.

SIGNIFICANT POINTS, OBJECTIVES AND EXERCISES

In this final chapter of the Teen Issues/Self-Esteem Program, some of the important points which have been previously covered will be reinforced. In addition, the group will focus on the actions they must take to start applying what they have learned. These exercises are directed at helping motivate the participants to implement their own personal action plans.

POINT #1

Making choices for oneself re-emphasizes the importance of making positive decisions and the value they can have upon one's future. One of the most valuable gifts parents can give their children is to help them become independent decision-makers. This is a gift they will use for the rest of their lives.

OBJECTIVE

To review:
  • the importance of making positive choices and decisions

LEADER'S NOTES

Exercise 1A involves the ability to make choices and decisions. Through these questions and the ones that follow, the participants will be asked to look at their ability to make choices for themselves and to develop an action plan for improving their lives. Sharing and discussion should be included at the conclusion of each written activity.

1. Why is it so important that you be able to make choices? What might cause a person to lose his/her ability to make choices?

2. In the story, Jamie makes a decision to take an action that changed his life, involving facing his fear in order to overcome it. The participants are asked to: Make a choice now to improve yourself and your life. and:
    (a) Describe what your choice involves
    (b) How will making this choice affect you?
    (c) When will you take the action to put your choice into effect? (Their agreement to take action, as in goal setting, must also include a time commitment).

EXERCISE #1
(A) The Ability to Make Choices

* * * *

POINT #2

The paragraph in the text that deals with belief systems, "Creating your reality through positive beliefs," states that "All aspects of your life are affected by your beliefs. The subconscious mind, like a computer, absorbs data that is offered to it and accepts it as fact. When either positive or negative beliefs are dominant, the subconscious mind directs that information into personal action reflecting the influence of that belief."

OBJECTIVE

To review:
- the group's understanding of how attitudes and beliefs affect outcome
- a plan of action involving a situation affected by their beliefs
- the use of affirmations

LEADER'S NOTES

Exercise 2A conveys information on how having a good attitude and using positive beliefs can affect the outcome of what one attempts. This exercise guides toward reframing any negative attitudes over an unsuccessful situation into believing in a positive way that outcomes can be altered. Group sharing should follow the written activities.

1. Describe a situation in your life in which the results have not been too satisfying. This could pertain to a relationship concern, school grades or any other situation you want to improve.

2. Describe how you might improve this situation using positive beliefs. Remove all your negative thoughts based on prior experience with this situation and approach it with the attitude that you will be able to achieve the results you want.

3. Even with a positive attitude, nothing much would happen unless the decision is made to take some form of action. The participants are asked to indicate what they will do as a first step in their action plan (for achieving a successful conclusion to their situation) and when they will take the first step. The time commitment is important; otherwise the action plan carries little meaning.

LEADER'S NOTES (continued)

Exercise 2B uses affirmations to change negative beliefs into positive beliefs. The discussion that takes place as a part of this exercise should involve what they have learned and feel in general about changing negative beliefs to positive ones and the use of affirmations.

1. Describe a belief you carry about yourself which is not positive and which you would like to change.

2. What would you like to change it to?

3. Write your own affirmation as if the change that you described in question 2 already takes place (present tense). Before proceeding with written affirmations, review what the text says about affirmations and how to use them (Chapter Seventeen, pages 167 through 170). Although the affirmations should be regarded as personal, anyone willing to share with the group, should be allowed to do so.

EXERCISE #2
(A) Your Attitude and Positive Beliefs Affect You
(B) Using Affirmations

*   *   *   *

POINT #3

All people are affected by pressure and stress at one time or another. The important thing to learn for oneself is how to handle and relieve the buildup of pressure and tension before it becomes destructive.

OBJECTIVE
To review:
   • what stress is and what to do about it

LEADER'S NOTES

Use this exercise to review the following issues, some of which have been previously covered with the group, regarding stress. Have them first write their answers to the first three activities and then follow up with group sharing. The first three issues covered are:

269

LEADER'S NOTES (continued)

1. Describe what you think stress is (an external or internal pressure) and the condition that results from that pressure.

2. List the three options for dealing with stress (described in Chapter Eight, Leader's Notes for Exercise 1).

3. How to relieve buildup of tension (covered in Chapter Six, Leader's Notes for Exercise 2C). Have the group brainstorm what they might do to relieve their buildup of stress, e.g., deep relaxation, listen to calming music, read a book, seek out help by speaking to someone about it, through sports, etc.

After the group discussion has been completed for the first three activities, have the participants write their responses to the last two issues which refer to stress in their lives, and what action they will take to improve their situation. The last two activities are:

4. Describe something that is currently stressful in your life.

5. What will you now do to deal with this situation?

The sharing of information that follows these activities can be non-specific (What have you learned from these exercises and any prior work covered on this subject that you might apply to how you deal with stress?) or specific responses to personal issues, based on the group's willingness to share.

EXERCISE #3
(A) How to Deal with Stress

* * * *

POINT #4

Plans are necessary for accomplishing any goal. Setting goals for oneself is a necessary tool for achieving what one wants to accomplish. However, goals alone will not accomplish what we want; we must also make a commitment to put the plan into action.

OBJECTIVE
To implement:
• a personal plan through goal-setting

LEADER'S NOTES

This exercise utilizes the information covered on goal-setting in Chapter Fifteen. It takes that information and puts it into a step-by-step procedure for the participants to use for developing their own goal and putting it into action.

It asks that they select a goal they would like to accomplish in approximately a year. This goal could be one of the goals they selected in the previous chapter or some other goal which is important to them. This exercise can help the group develop a positive action plan for themselves.

EXERCISE #4

(A) Your Plan for Achievement

CLOSURE

The following closure statement is included in the *Student Workbook* at the end of their exercises. It is important they be congratulated and recognized for their participation in this program.

You have completed a lot of work as a part of this program. Although it may be a different kind of work than you have been used to, it's the kind of learning that can help people grow and improve their personal lives. If you have gained some new insights that may move you in a more positive way toward achieving happiness or you have learned more about yourself, then you should feel proud, for you have accomplished something of great value.

Congratulations on completing this Teen Issues/Self-Esteem Program. Continue to make good choices for yourself as you follow your road to happiness and success.

*   *   *   *

(A) The Ability to Make Choices

In the last two chapters of the text, some important issues are covered again for your review. They include:

1. The ability to make choices (decisions) is critical to your future.

(a) Why is it so important that you be able to make choices (decisions)?

(b)What might cause a person to lose his/her ability to make choices?

2. In the story, Jamie makes a decision to take an action that changed his life; it involves facing his fear in order to overcome it. Make a choice now to improve yourself and your life.

(a) Describe what your choice involves:

(b) How will making this choice affect you?

(c) When will you take the first action to put your choice into effect?

* * * *

(A) Your Attitude and Positive Beliefs Affect You

By now you must realize that your attitude towards other people, yourself, and life in general sets you up for how happy and successful you will be.

Your attitude includes how you view and approach your experiences. If you enter into situations with positive beliefs, feeling you can accomplish your task, you stand a much better chance of doing so than if you believed the outcome was going to be a negative one. It's a simple process that actually works, but how often do you use it?

1. For this exercise, think about and describe something in your life in which the results have not been satisfying to you. Have you been approaching this situation in a negative way instead of believing it will come out the way you want it to? The situation could apply to your relationship with your parents, your friends, or something else in your life that you would like to improve.

Describe your situation:

2. Now, take the situation you just described in question 1. Think about how you might improve upon it, if you began to believe in a positive way that you could do so. Describe how you might improve your situation with positive beliefs.

I will improve my situation by doing the following:

3. Nothing will happen to change your situation even with positive beliefs unless you are willing to put your new plan into action. In this activity using the same situation from above, describe your plan of action. Include what you intend to do as the first step of your action plan and when you will start to do it.

What I will do:
When I will start my action plan:

(B) Using Affirmations

The text states, "The subconscious mind, like a computer, absorbs information that is offered to it and accepts it as fact. Your actions or behaviors, connected to your belief system, remain with you until they are displaced by stronger beliefs." Affirmations are positive declarations made to oneself. Using affirmations is a method for developing and inputting new beliefs.

In this exercise, you are to select a not-so-positive belief about yourself which you would like to change. Write an affirmation to help produce the change.

1. Describe the belief that you would like to change:

2. What would you like to change it to?

```
_____
_____
_____
_____
_____
_____
_____
_____
```

3. Write your positive affirmation as if the change you would like to make has already taken place. Refer to what you described in question 2. Before you begin, you may review what your text says about affirmations and how to use them, covered in Chapter Seventeen, pages 167 through 170.

```
_____
_____
_____
_____
_____
_____
_____
```

Now that you have completed your affirmation, it is important to remember that for it to produce change, you must use it. The portion of the text which you reviewed tells you how to use your affirmation.

*　　*　　*　　*

(A) How to Deal with Stress

This is an extremely important subject because stress, if handled properly, can actually be helpful to you. However, if it is not dealt with in a correct manner it can produce a lot of damage.

Questions 1 through 3 are for group review of what you have learned regarding stress.

Issues For Discussion

1. Describe what you think stress is:

2. List the three options for dealing with stress:

1.
2.
3.

3. List three things you might do to relieve the buildup of tension:

1.
2.
3.

Do not go on to questions 4 and 5 until the discussion has been completed for 1 through 3.

4. Describe something that is currently stressful to you in your life:

5. What will you now do to deal with this stressful situation?

*   *   *   *

(A) Your Plan for Achievement

DEVELOPING A GOAL
YOUR PERSONAL PLAN FOR ACHIEVEMENT

Use the information covered in Chapter Fifteen and the following form to develop a goal for yourself. It should be something you would like to accomplish for yourself in approximately one year from now (long-term), with as many short-term goals as you feel will be necessary to keep you working towards your goal. Select a goal to be accomplished within a year. You can use a goal that you selected in the prior chapter or some other goal that is important to you.

(a) Describe your goal and what you want to accomplish:

```
_____
_____
_____
_____
```

(b) Why do you want to accomplish this goal? (purpose or reason) It is important to be aware of what accomplishing this goal means to you.

```
_____
_____
_____
_____
```

(c) Can you achieve this goal? _____ If yes, continue. If not, you should either question your attitude regarding why you feel you couldn't accomplish your goal (your own fears or a negative attitude may be your major barrier) or select another goal.

(d) List any barriers, things that might cause you problems in accomplishing your goal, and what you might do to overcome those barriers.

Barriers	What you can do to overcome the barriers

(e) When taking a long trip with a limited amount of time (like going on vacation), it is important to know when you will arrive at your final destination. In order to get there on time, so that you enjoy yourself and then be back home when you need to be, you would need to keep track of the progress of your trip.

That trip is like your long-term goal. The in-between stops are your tasks or short-term goals. Keeping track of where and when you're going to stop for the night is like your measurement or completion dates for your tasks.

Home   *   *   *   *   *   *Vacation destination
   * In between stops every 350 miles (approximately every 6 hours)

(f) Prepare a list of the important tasks (short-term goals) you will need to complete in order to reach your goal. Start with the task to be done first; then list the dates when you think you can complete the task. The third column can be left open for now. Later, list the actual dates when you complete these tasks.

The tasks you list are short-term goals on the road to your long-term goal.

Task	Estimated completion date	Actual completion date

(g) Now that you have developed your task and estimated completion dates, you are ready for the next step, estimating your completion date for your overall goal. Using the date for the completion of your last task as a guide, list an estimated date for completing and accomplishing your major goal. Goals must use some form of measurement, otherwise they are easily ignored and forgotten. The measurement of your goal is there to help you, so make it realistic (one you can reach).

Month	Day	Year

(h) You're now ready to start working at accomplishing your goal.

- Work on one task at a time.
- Keep track of how you're doing by writing the completion dates for each of the tasks as they are accomplished.
- If any barriers or obstacles come up along the way, use your personal strength and your desire to complete your goal to remove them.
- Working towards a goal shows self-motivation; be proud of yourself.
- When you've reached your goal, reward yourself, for you deserve it!

CLOSURE

You have completed a lot of work as a part of this program. Although it may be a different kind of work than you have been used to, it's the kind of learning that can help people grow and improve their personal lives. If you have gained some new insights that may move you in a more positive way toward achieving happiness or you have learned more about yourself, then you should feel proud, for you have accomplished something of great value.

Congratulations on completing this Teen Issues/Self-Esteem Program. Continue to make good choices for yourself as you follow your road to happiness and success.

*   *   *   *

INDEX

NUMBERS AFTER TOPICS REFER TO CHAPTERS

ORDER FORM

MONROE PRESS
16107 Gledhill Street, Suite 187
Sepulveda, California 91343-2918
(818) 891-6464

Please send me the following by Dr. Monte Elchoness:

QUANTITY	TITLE	PRICE	TOTAL
_____	Why Can't Anyone Hear Me? $10.95		_____
_____	Guide to Adolescent Enrichment 16.95		_____
_____	Teen Issues Student Workbook 4.95		_____
_____	Sigmund Says 6.95		_____
_____	Stress Reduction Training Deep Relaxation Audio Tape 9.00		_____

Tax: California residents only, add 6% tax   _____

Shipping & Handling: 10% of order ($2.00 minimum)   _____

TOTAL AMOUNT ENCLOSED $_____

Name _____

School/Organization _____

Address _____

City _____ State _____ Zip _____